INCONVENIENT
Parenting

INCONVENIENT

Parenting

ACTIVATE
YOUR CHILD'S
GOD-GIVEN TRAITS

Melissa Hannigan

MOODY PUBLISHERS
CHICAGO

Edited by Amanda Cleary Eastep
Interior design: Ragont Design
Cover design: Christopher Tobias and Erik M. Peterson
Cover painting of watercolor background copyright © 2023 by Rawpixel.com/Adobe Stock (227224314). All rights reserved.

ISBN: 978-0-8024-3124-0

Originally delivered by fleets of horse-drawn wagons, the affordable paperbacks from D. L. Moody's publishing house resourced the church and served everyday people. Now, after more than 125 years of publishing and ministry, Moody Publishers' mission remains the same—even if our delivery systems have changed a bit. For more information on other books (and resources) created from a biblical perspective, go to www.moodypublishers.com or write to:

Moody Publishers
820 N. LaSalle Boulevard
Chicago, IL 60610

1 3 5 7 9 10 8 6 4 2

Printed in the United States of America

My greatest gifts and joy in this world:
Joey, Maddy, Ella, and Charlotte.
I would not trade all the conveniences of this life
for the privilege of parenting you.

Contents

Foreword   9

Introduction   13

1. What Is Inconvenient Parenting?   17

2. Wisdom   25

3. Wonder   35

4. Vitality   49

5. Sensitivity   59

6. Flexibility   71

7. Curiosity   83

8. Creativity   97

9. Imagination   105

10. Inventiveness   115

11. Playfulness   121

12. Humor   127

13. Joy   133

You Can Do It!   141

Acknowledgments   143

Notes   147

Foreword

My dolls' bunkbeds became a double-decker bus after my grandmother, mom, and aunt took my female cousins and me to downtown Milwaukee to ride on one. I thought the bus was the best thing ever! We all sat on the second level, and in my young mind, I thought I could see forever. The unique experience stuck with me, and I wanted my dolls to have this kind of fun, too.

After that fun day, my mom sometimes played "bus" with me. She never said, "Kathy, these beds don't move. What do you mean we're going on a trip?" I will be forever grateful that she honored my imagination. She stimulated my curiosity by asking questions about what we saw on our trip. She engaged in my wonder as I "oohed" and "aahed" at all we saw. Together, we experienced great joy!

I played school so much with stuffed animals, dolls, and young neighbors that I should have earned a degree. My dad wasn't a fan of the chalkdust created as I used the chalkboard on wheels, but he let me use it. He was an engineer and allowed me to use some of his graph paper and special pencils. I still love both and have an engineering pencil among my pens and pencils in a container to my right as I type this foreword. He supported my dreams, creativity, growing wisdom, and flexibility, and I will be forever grateful.

My parents wouldn't have said they were inconvenienced by my playtimes or my brother's science experiments. Sometimes I know we were too loud and had too many things everywhere. I'm grateful for my parents and all parents who honor their children and childhood and know play matters.

Melissa Hannigan does this. She is passionate that her four children have a healthy childhood experience so they can become who God created them to be. This is one of the reasons she's the right person to write this book. In addition, she earned a master's degree in Christian counseling and has had many experiences as a conference speaker, volunteering with teens at church, and serving as a court-appointed guardian ad litem as a voice for foster children.

I've known Melissa, her husband, John, and their children for several years. We have had many deep conversations and fun times together—yes, the children and adults! I'm grateful for their friendship and that Melissa and John are part of the Celebrate Kids' leadership, speaking, and writing team.

You can trust Melissa and her ideas. She makes a strong case for valuing each trait and explains why and how allowing your children to use them will enhance learning and life. She demonstrates and teaches how to put children first without enabling them to become self-centered, arrogant, and selfish. She encourages you to be willing to be inconvenienced so you can live abundant, joyful lives together. These traits help your children thrive!

And your son, who makes messes experimenting with whatever he finds, might become a well-respected clinical chemist. And your school-playing daughter might have fun memories of riding on double-decker buses in several countries and also serve God as a teacher, speaker, and writer.

Today matters. Be willing to be inconvenienced!

KATHY KOCH, PhD
Founder, Celebrate Kids, Inc.
Founding Associate, Ignite the Family

Introduction

When I was a little girl, I loved books. I would spend hours in the library picking out books and even more hours huddled in a chair somewhere reading them. My younger sister would get irritated with me because I had my nose stuck in a book instead of playing games or talking with her. If you would have told me all those years ago that I would be writing a book one day, I might have believed you; I dreamed of writing someday. But if you had told me I would be a married, forty-year-old mom of four kids writing a *parenting* book, I definitely would have laughed. I was strictly a fiction kind of girl, thank you very much! The whole book writing process has been a dream. Not without its challenges—there have been some difficulties and insecurities that I've had to overcome—but it has been a miracle in progress.

I want to share with you a little about this miracle and how I know that God alone has brought me to this place and this book being in your hands.

In 2019, while attending a local homeschool conference, my husband, John, and I were shopping in the vendor hall at the end of the first day when we ran into author and speaker Dr. Kathy Koch, founder of Celebrate Kids, Inc. I knew a little about this expert on parenting, but I didn't know that Kathy's and my husband's paths had crossed years before when John was still a teenager. Reconnecting with Kathy at the conference set all our paths in a new direction. John was consulting for businesses, and Kathy was in need of some fresh ideas and vision for her Celebrate Kids organization.

As John began to work with Kathy, I benefited from her extensive knowledge. God used several books written by Kathy to help shape our family in important ways. Spring of 2020 hit, and moms and dads across the globe scrambled to find ways to parent their children well amid a global pandemic, lockdowns, and new anxieties. God knew that John and I needed Kathy's wisdom for our family to not only endure but thrive in that season.

During the pandemic, Dr. Kathy introduced me to the twelve genius qualities identified by Thomas Armstrong in his book *Awakening Genius in the Classroom*. Curiosity, playfulness, imagination, creativity, wonder, wisdom, inventiveness, vitality, sensitivity, flexibility, humor, and joy were the twelve qualities he identified as integral in helping children reach their fullest potential.[1] He wasn't suggesting that every child would have a genius level IQ but that they all had untapped potential. I was desperate for some fresh inspiration and ideas that would bring some joy back into our homeschool days, and I definitely wanted to help my children reach their fullest potential. I embraced these qualities and began to prioritize them in our home. A few of the qualities were natural for us; creativity and inventiveness, for example, were part of our normal routine. I was naturally gifted in some, like sensitivity, and John naturally exhibited others, like a sense of humor and playfulness. We even found some new qualities that we all needed to work on, like flexibility.

In 2021, I was given opportunities to speak at some national conferences about the many ways these twelve qualities have influenced our home. Parents from Virginia to Alaska resonated with these ideas. I am so encouraged when I hear from other parents who have found these ideas helpful. My prayer is that you too will be inspired as you read these words and learn about these qualities—not because I have all the answers, but because I believe God has given me something that can impact your family too!

I want you to know up front that I do not write these words from a place of having arrived as the perfect parent. None of us will ever be a perfect parent. We will not get it right all the time. I certainly do not! But I wholeheartedly believe we are the perfect parents for the children God has entrusted to us. My prayer is that you will fully embrace the role God has given you and you will see how these qualities can help unlock your child's full potential. I know too that we can rest in the knowledge that even when we mess up, God's grace can fill in the gaps. Our job is to turn to Him and trust Him to work all things together for good in our homes, in our lives, and in our families. I am a strong believer in the God of the Bible. My perspective on the world, parenting, and the future is shaped by my biblical worldview first and foremost. I think it is only fair to let you know that primarily, I am a Jesus-loving mom who just happened to stumble onto these qualities that have helped change my family for the better. What I've found has been such a gift to us, and I want to continue to pass this on to others!

Whether you are a working parent, stay-at-home parent, or work-from-home parent, this book is for you. You may be single or divorced, a blended family or foster family. You may be a homeschool family, a public school family, or any combination of the above. The truths in this book are for you! No matter what kind of family you are, no matter how unique your children are (and they are all so different), you can benefit from recognizing and nurturing these twelve qualities. Just be prepared to be a little—okay, maybe a lot—inconvenienced when you choose to prioritize these qualities in your home.

Chapter 1

What Is Inconvenient Parenting?

To the world, we may have seemed to have it all. We lived in Houston, and John had a great paying job. I was able to stay home with the kids if I wanted. We had the beautiful big house, brand-new cars, private school for the kids, the nanny to help with the babies, the house cleaner, the yard guy, and the open line of credit at the high-end department stores. I could buy all the organic groceries I wanted without ever wondering if we had enough in the bank account to afford it. We could go out to dinner or order takeout any time I didn't feel like cooking. Our life was all about convenience and ease. So why in the world was I asking God to do whatever it took to get my family away from there? I probably sound crazy, right?

If you had asked me then why I prayed those prayers, I would have said it was because I knew God wanted more for our family. While from the outside it may have looked as though we had it all together, I knew that on the inside we were struggling. John was always on the road for work, and we never had time for a family meal. The two older kids were so busy with their schoolwork and outside activities that we were rarely all at the same place at the same time. An attitude of entitlement began to creep into our home, a false belief that money and success were the most important things in life. When one of our children began bragging about his father's invite-only credit card and how he could have a helicopter pick him up from school if he wanted, I knew something had to change. So, I began to pray, "Whatever it takes Lord, remove us from this place!"

God answered those prayers. He took us from Houston in a pretty painful way. But He opened our eyes to a much better life for our family. The world would not say it was better, but *we* know it is. Today, we do not have the luxuries and conveniences we had back in Houston. But we have more family meals together, more family time, a better perspective of what really matters, and a clearer understanding of God's purpose for our family and for each one of us. This purpose is rarely convenient but always worth it.

You may be wondering, what exactly is inconvenient parenting?

A parent who is willing to be inconvenienced is a parent who is willing to do the hard and holy sacrificial work of raising children to reach the potential and purpose God has for them.

Elisabeth Elliot wrote that "the measure of our love is the measure of our willingness to be inconvenienced."[1] The idea of being inconvenienced is not an easy one. It means sacrifice, giving up what's easy for what's better. It's a willingness to tolerate some messes, messy kitchen tables, and messy conversations. It's taking the harder, less traveled way knowing that it's all worth it in the long run. It's dying to ourselves and putting our family's needs before our own, at times knowing that the reward of seeing our children become who God created them to be is worth all the effort and inconvenience. That was what I knew God wanted for our family, all those years ago in Houston.

Inconvenient parenting means parents keep the end goal in mind, understanding that the goal of parenting is to equip their children to fulfill the unique purposes and plans God has for each child. Sometimes that means sacrificing short-term comfort for long-term success. That has been our story. It has gotten much less comfortable in our home. Where we had thousands of extra square feet in our old house, we now squeeze into much tighter quarters. But we have richer relationships, many more great conversations, and a lot more laughter.

It wasn't just giving up of our life in Houston that led to these changes, but a way of igniting our family to reaching its God-given potential. I am excited to introduce you to the twelve qualities that have impacted our family. When Thomas Armstrong first identified the "qualities of a genius," he described traits that, when encouraged, unlocked a student's greatest potential for growth.[2] The qualities—curiosity, playfulness, imagination, creativity, wonder, wisdom, inventiveness, vitality, sensitivity, flexibility, humor, and joy—were introduced to me by Dr. Kathy in a workshop in which she described ways that homeschool families could integrate them into their school days. Immediately, I resonated with these traits. Many of them—like wisdom, inventiveness, wonder, imagination, and creativity—were qualities I was already trying to instill in our children.

At first, my husband John was oblivious to the changes I was implementing. Our kitchen table was covered with the latest invention or craft project. His mismatched socks were repurposed as doll clothes and sock puppets. He could not understand why I was willing to stop at every tiny thing that caught one of the children's attention when we would go for family walks in the neighborhood. To him, a crawling caterpillar was not a big deal, but to my daughter, who took notice and wondered how many legs it had and why it was crawling so slowly and where it lived and did I think it had a family, this was an opportunity to experience wonder and curiosity. I tried to explain to John what I was beginning to understand, that these "genius qualities" were really so much more than what Armstrong described as keys to unlocking academic achievement; they were God-given qualities that were helping us to fully embrace our abundant life.

One day our family was on the last leg of a several-hour-long road trip. The two youngest daughters were joyfully and loudly singing (off-key) a song that they'd made up on the spot. I don't know if you have children who make up songs, but sometimes they can be pretty cute . . . and sometimes they can be pretty annoying. On this particular day, the song was not cute. But as their song continued from the back, I sat up front in the passenger seat, unfazed by their off-tune warbling. I assumed that John was getting ready to tell them to be quiet, to stop singing, or to pick another song.

Instead, he looked at me and said, "I get it. I get why you let them do this. You're allowing them to be creative and musical and imaginative, just the way God created them to be."

Maybe it was his new position as executive director of Celebrate Kids, where he was around Dr. Kathy and her wealth of knowledge about children and raising them to be who God created them to be. Maybe it was my recent excitement over the genius qualities and his front row seat to the change that was taking place in our home. But in that moment, I knew that our family would never be the same; we would always prioritize each of these qualities because we both understood the value it was having in our family, even though John was just beginning to understand how inconvenient it might be at times.

As we drove, I asked him to tell me what other ways he had noticed changes in our home. More messes, more creative projects, more walks to stare at God's creation (especially at sunset, because those are my favorite). He brought up the time I let the kids make a stained-glass painting on the kitchen window and what a hassle it was to remove the tape and paint.

"Isn't it more work for you, though? More messes to clean up?" he asked. He knew that housecleaning was my least favorite thing.

"Yes. But it's worth it, don't you think?" I answered.

"True, but does it have to be so inconvenient?"

I believe it does. But I also believe you will agree it's worth it! It may take some extra work, extra supplies to keep around the house, maybe even extra tears from difficult conversations you would rather skip altogether. It will definitely take saying no to good things in order to make time for the best things, and possibly changing your family priorities, although maybe not as drastically as our move from Houston. The sacrifices you make to ignite and nurture these traits will help your children become who God created them to be.

As we explore each of the twelve qualities, I am going to show you why they are necessary and how you can begin to recognize and encourage them in your family. I will also point out some ways that we might inadvertently discourage them and what you can do instead.

I'll explain from a biblical perspective where I believe Armstrong's definitions of these qualities fall short. His research and explanations on this topic have been foundational; however, my view of Creator God informs my view that all twelve of these qualities are given to everyone, to differing degrees, in order that we may fully engage with God and the world He created, so that we are able to fulfill the purposes He has for each of us.

Are you ready to dive into the qualities and learn how your family can benefit from them, like we did? I am excited for you to find your unique ways to incorporate these for your children's benefit. I will share ideas of what worked for us and for others, but remember, you are the one God chose to parent your children, and you are the one best equipped to decide what will work in your home. I hope you are ready to get a little inconvenienced for the good of your kids!

Chapter 2

Wisdom

Close your eyes and imagine your children five, ten, twenty years from now. Picture their sweet little faces maturing into adulthood. Envision how much taller they've grown. Dream, for a moment, about their future spouses, future children, and your grandchildren. How will they parent? Will they grow up to love God and embrace who He created them to be? Will they know how to discern between truth and almost truth? Will they be wise?

While we don't have much control over how tall our children will become or how much facial hair they may grow or how many children they may have, we do have influence over how wise they become.

Wisdom is foundational to everything else that will follow in this book. I believe that wisdom is more precious than jewels and nothing that we desire for our children compares.[1] Charles Spurgeon preached that "wisdom is man's true path—that which enables him to accomplish best the end of his being, and which, therefore, gives to him the richest enjoyment, and the fullest play for all his powers."[2] Isn't that what we want for our children?

If we agree that we want our children to accomplish their purposes and enjoy this full, abundant life, then the path of wisdom is the way. But what do I mean by wisdom?

WHAT IS WISDOM?

If you look up the definition of wisdom, you will find different meanings. The *Oxford English Dictionary* defines wisdom as the "capacity of judging rightly in matters relating to life and conduct."[3] *Merriam-Webster* defines wisdom as an "ability to discern inner qualities and relationships," "insight," "good sense," or "judgment."[4] And Dictionary.com defines it as "the quality or state of being wise; knowledge of what is true or right coupled with just judgment as to action."[5] Thomas Armstrong defines wisdom as experiencing wonder of the world directly, without a filter. Armstrong saw wisdom as an eyes-wide-open receptiveness to the world.[6] And this is observable in childhood.

Have you ever taken a young child to a fair, a park, or a beach and watched as they stare wide-eyed, their mouths slightly open, soaking in everything? By adulthood, we seem to become immune to the everyday wonders around us; but childhood is a period of rapid brain development. Much neurobiological research over the past twenty years supports the idea that early childhood experiences influence brain growth.[7] This is exactly the way God created us to function. And God knew way back at creation that as He shaped humanity with this drive toward experiences, it is the first step toward learning new things. But is that all wisdom is?

Each of these definitions highlight aspects of wisdom, which include experience, knowledge, discernment, and judgment. I call this human wisdom. This wisdom has its place as it helps us navigate the world with knowledge and understanding. Christians, however, believe that ultimate wisdom comes from God.

John Piper, in his sermon "How to Get Wisdom," differentiates between human wisdom and God's wisdom. He explains that human wisdom is factual knowledge, situational insight, and necessary resolve. These encompass the traditional definitions of wisdom, but only God's wisdom is infallible.[8] I think it's important to make this distinction. Human wisdom is beneficial for our children, but God's wisdom should be our ultimate goal. This is why, while I appreciate Armstrong's definition, we must broaden our view of wisdom.

If our goal for our child is to simply learn new information and understand how to properly apply that wisdom, then we would only be tapping into the world's understanding of wisdom. Our goal must be for them to grow in understanding so that they may live with good judgment and discernment. But who defines "good judgment"? If we are not seeking God's wisdom directly from His Word, then "good" becomes relative to opinion and culture. I want my children going to the source of unchanging wisdom to define what is good.

In today's culture of fake news and easy access to whatever society calls "truth," our kids must discern actual truth, and wisely apply that truth to their lives. This type of wisdom starts with an understanding of the inerrancy of God's truth. This is the heart of godly wisdom, to discern what God says is true and apply it properly.

How do we teach wisdom to our kids?

Wisdom starts with humility. We must first admit that we need help because we don't possess wisdom within ourselves. We must be willing to be a student, desiring to learn and grow in knowledge. We never get to a place where we have learned everything we need to know, right? Modeling this type of humility to our children is an important first step.

We must hunger for knowing more about the world around us, and especially God's Word. Do you have a hobby, or have you learned a new skill? Is there a Bible study that you have enjoyed lately? Have you demonstrated to your kids that you desire to keep learning and growing, or are you content believing that you already know everything you need to know? If you're reading this book, then you are demonstrating a desire to learn and to grow. That's a great example to your kids!

I learned in the last ten years how to crochet. My children witnessed my frustrating beginning and pitiful first attempts at scarves and baby blankets. But they also witnessed me grow and develop in my ability, mostly through seeking more experienced friends who helped me along the way. Also, thanks to YouTube, I was able to teach myself some new crocheting skills. I hope my kids understand that this mom still has a lot to learn, and I am humbly willing to admit that and willing to put in the time and effort to continue to learn.

For you, it may not be crocheting; it could be birdwatching, tennis, or even the history of ancient Egypt that you're learning alongside your kids as they study. As a homeschool mom, I get a lot of opportunities to say, "I don't know, let's research that!" My family is not under any delusion that I know everything, but they do know that what I don't know, I can learn. More is caught than taught, and if we demonstrate an ongoing interest in learning, our kids will catch the excitement for learning too.

Ultimately, we want our children to see us going to the source of all wisdom. They need to see us seeking God's Word for wisdom and direction. They need to hear us talk about what God is teaching us because we must never stop learning and growing, especially when it comes to the living and active Word of God. If we desire our children to seek godly wisdom above all, then they must see us doing that as well.

Maybe that means you occasionally include your children in your time of Scripture study. It may be more convenient to do your studying in private—trust me, I love my quiet time alone, but modeling this habit before your family, no matter how noisy it may be, helps them see the value that you place on God's Word.

But we cannot simply stop at showing our children the importance of learning new things. That is only the first step toward wisdom. They must also see us seeking to apply that knowledge with discernment. They need to see us taking what we are learning in God's Word and applying it in our daily lives. They need to hear us talking about relying on the Holy Spirit for discernment and praying for strength to implement whatever God is asking us to change. No matter the age of your children, they will benefit from seeing a parent who humbly seeks God for truth and then shares about the ways they are applying that truth! This is true wisdom!

How do we empower our children to seek out truth?

The first step is to become students of our kids and discover how they learn best. In her book *8 Great Smarts*,[9] Dr. Kathy describes the eight ways children learn. She calls these different learning styles their "smarts" because it describes the natural way that they are wired to receive information. Some children are music smart and love listening to different genres of music or using instruments from other cultures—these children will be inspired to learn in musical ways. Another child will thrive outside in nature—being surrounded by creation, and therefore an outdoor environment, makes learning more engaging for them. Our job as parents is to figure out how they are wired to encourage their unique style of learning. When we understand how our children are created uniquely it becomes much easier to create settings for learning.

Another great step in helping our children become wise is to introduce them to various ideas and information. Charlotte Mason, a pioneer in early childhood education in the 1900s, believed that a child's mind was just as hungry as their stomach and that a parent's job is to provide variety for them to feast on.[10] This feasting will look different depending on the stage of your child's development.

When our children are babies, we can provide visually stimulating environments, talk to them often, play music, and read picture books to them. Elementary-age children are eager to learn new things; for parents, this is an ideal time to capitalize on this desire. Read engaging stories, find out what they are interested in, and learn about it together. We went through a period where one child was fascinated by the *Titanic*. We read books, studied the history of the era, and watched documentaries. These activities reinforce the message that in our home, when we are interested in a topic, we will study about it together!

This is also the perfect time to help your children learn how to identify reputable sources of information. Wisdom is not just the gathering of facts but involves discerning where to go for that information and what to do with that knowledge. This is something we must intentionally teach our children.

By the teenage years and into young adulthood, children should understand where to go for reputable truth and scholarly sources. Hopefully by this point, they understand the value of God's Word and its infallibility. We must help them develop a biblical worldview that stands firm on the unchanging Word of God. Once their worldview is firm, it is time to encourage studying a variety of cultures and viewpoints that don't necessarily align with their worldview. Invite people of different cultures and views into your home and learn more about them. Help your teen learn how to think critically about current events. They must be able to defend their faith, so introducing apologetics is helpful. Encourage your young teen to travel. Mission trips are a great way to see that the world is so much bigger than they realized. Even if your family can't physically go anywhere, there are boundless resources that can transport us to foreign lands. The point is to help our children value understanding and insight.

It seems so simple, right? Just model a love of learning, expose them to lots of valuable information to feast on, help them develop a strong biblical worldview that filters all things through the lens of Scripture, and they will be wise. Okay, maybe that doesn't sound simple, but it is doable. So why aren't we as Christian parents doing a better job of this?

(I'm looking in the mirror when I ask this.) May I gently suggest that while we have the best of intentions, we let lesser things distract us?

What gets in the way of wisdom?

Laying out a feast of information for our children takes intentionality and time. We can have the best of intentions, but if we don't prioritize time with our children, we won't be able to influence them toward wisdom. Whether you chose to educate at home, public school, or private school, parents are the primary influencers of education, especially in the early years. But if our schedules are so jam-packed with activities, then we won't be able to impact our families.

Modeling humility, prioritizing God's Word, providing exposure to new ideas and cultures—it all takes intention and presence. I told you up front that this type of parenting will be inconvenient. It is sacrificial to clear our schedules; to lay down what we want to do so that we can do what we need to do. I don't always want to read a book about the *Titanic* for the sixteenth time with my child instead of watching my favorite show, but I do it. Are there things that you can lay down in order to show up?

Could it be your family's dependence on technology that eats away at your quality time?

Technology has given us all access to a lot of information, but also makes us all more selfish. We spend time on our devices playing what we want, looking up articles that we want to read, and reinforcing the false belief that we are "the center of [our] own universe."[11] We will talk a lot about the dangers of technology, but right now I want you to think about your own technology use. Do you choose the immediate satisfaction of scrolling on social media instead of sitting in silence and being available to your child? Do your children go into their own rooms, with their own devices, to watch their preferred entertainment? We all do this from time to time, but what if we chose instead to spend that time together? What if we read a book together as a family or watched a documentary on a topic of interest and then talked about it? What if we studied God's Word together and shared how the Holy Spirit was working in our lives? This is what inconvenient parenting looks like. This is how we are intentional about pointing our children toward wisdom.

In addition to creating an environment that supports quality time, parents must also provide a safe place for children to learn from their mistakes. Sometimes opportunities to apply knowledge in real-world ways can lead to mistakes, and mistakes are some of the best teachers. But how often do we get frustrated by our children's mistakes? As a recovering perfectionist, this is an area I struggle with! Thankfully, I have had wonderful mentors in my life who have helped me to find the growth that comes from making mistakes.

My girls are always in the kitchen trying new recipes. And that always provides opportunities to learn. On one particular day, they decided following a recipe was unnecessary. And much to everyone's shock, the masterpiece didn't turn out how they expected. They learned a valuable lesson in the importance of following the recipe, especially when it comes to baking. Now, I could have gotten frustrated with them for wasting ingredients and making the house smell like burned pancakes, and to be honest, in the past that is what I would've done. But instead, I saw this mistake as a chance to talk about wisdom and why it is important to listen to those who know more than we do.

Our kids are going to mess up. As parents, we have to allow room for our children to experience the impact of those mistakes in the safety of our homes, so that they grow in wisdom and understanding. Someday they will leave our homes, and if they have not learned the importance of wisdom, the consequences of their actions could be severe.

We want our kids to value wisdom throughout their lives—both man's wisdom and especially God's wisdom. So, let's prioritize wisdom, model to our kids how vital it is to never stop learning, never stop experiencing new and challenging things, and give them space to put that knowledge into practice. It won't be easy, but it will definitely be worth it!

Chapter 3

WONDER

Our family of six loves to travel. Even when our teenagers were just little babies in a baby carrier strapped to us or in a double stroller beside older siblings, we took all our children on trips. Friends and family thought we were nuts for spending money on trips with young ones who would not remember them. But we were undeterred. From our very first family trip with our very first baby, we understood that while a child might not recall details from our travels, they were still learning and experiencing the world right alongside us. And that was far more valuable than all the money in the world.

Joey, our oldest, was only a few months old on that first trip. I was a young, new mom who was worried about all the details that come with traveling with an infant. Diaper bags, nursing covers, and a bulky stroller were just a few of the *essential* items. And don't forget the aforementioned baby carrier: a crazy-complicated apparatus I had not yet perfected putting on myself, let alone maneuvering a wiggling infant into! I can still picture my young mom self, sweating and getting frustrated as I tried to strap that thing on while my sweet husband looked on, offering guidance and support but also avoiding becoming the target of my frustrations. On top of all that stress, I faced the anxiety that came with needing to find a place to nurse every three hours and the fear that I might need something for my baby I could not get (as if we were on a remote island without stores on every corner). To put it bluntly, I had not been looking forward to that trip; in fact, I'd been dreading it. Boy, did travel become inconvenient once the baby came along!

John, on the other hand, was eager and excited for our first big trip with our little one. He has always loved traveling, and he couldn't wait to do so with our son. Where I saw details and stress, worries and inconveniences, John saw adventure, excitement, and opportunity. This is a good picture of how differently we look at life. (I mean, one of us has to worry about the details, right?) I am so thankful for John's optimistic perspective on life because our family would have missed many opportunities to experience new and exciting things if it hadn't been for John's willingness to jump into life without hesitation—inconveniences and all.

That first vacation, and so many family trips since then, have been amazing, memory-making times for us. Trips allow us to slow down, get out of our normal routine, and notice the world around us. I wouldn't call those trips vacations, because they were certainly not relaxing, but I wouldn't trade those memories for all the conveniences in the world!

WHAT IS WONDER?

Sometimes it takes getting out of our daily routine for us to notice the magic, the wonder, that is already right in front of us. And that is exactly what that first family trip did for us. It set us on a path that allows this adventure-loving, trip-taking, memory-making family to prioritize getting out of our daily ruts and routines to experience the magic of the world around us!

Have you ever gone to a new place and stood in awe of some part of creation? John and I recently got away alone to Colorado for our anniversary. Cuddled together on the cog railway, we enjoyed the hour-long ride to the top of Pikes Peak. At the foot of the mountain, we saw dense forests and lots of birds and squirrels, and each level of incline revealed views of different types of trees. The further up the mountain we progressed, the sparser the foliage and more expansive the views. The railway conductor kept reminding us to drink plenty of water because the air grew thinner, and our lungs worked harder at this elevation. Once we finally reached the apex of the mountain, the view was almost indescribable. The world below looked so very small; the clouds appeared so close we could touch them. Emerald blues of nearby lakes sparkled like tiny gems in the distance. Rocky brown mountain ranges appeared to be only small hills a child could build with dirt. The world seemed to blend together where you couldn't tell where the ground ended and the sky began. God's creation was on majestic display.

The awe and wonder overwhelmed us. Did you know that view was the inspiration for author Katherine Lee Bates as she penned the words to "America the Beautiful"? I know firsthand how awe-inspiring it truly is! And that is exactly the way God created us to respond to creation, with awe and wonder! The Psalms are filled with worship inspired by the heavens, which declare the glory of God.[1] Psalm 65 says, "The pastures of the wilderness drip, and the hills encircle themselves with rejoicing. The meadows are clothed with flocks and the valleys are covered with grain; they shout for joy, yes, they sing" (vv. 12–13). Can you picture those pastures and hills? Don't those images make you want to rejoice in God's glory in creation?

It turns out there are many benefits to experiencing wonder, especially in nature. God our Creator made us to respond to creation not only emotionally but chemically as well!

First, we will talk about the emotional benefits. According to research published in the *Journal of Personality and Social Psychology*, when we allow ourselves and our kids to be in awe of the beauty of nature, it causes us to be more invested in the well-being of others, more generous, and less entitled.[2] That is incredible! Awe of nature can make us less self-centered and more compassionate. This is something we all want for our children, right? The God-given quality of wonder inside us can help our kids to be more aware of the world around them.

Wonder causes our children—and us—to see that we are all a small part of a huge masterpiece. Standing on the summit of Pikes Peak, seeing the vastness of the bigger world, I felt that smallness. Wonder gives us time to pause, consider, question, and reflect. When we are in awe, we notice something bigger than ourselves, something that points to a Creator who is worthy of worship.

Besides making us more others-focused, being in nature has positive effects on our well-being and emotional health. There are restorative properties in nature because of the order found there. Nature provides people time to step away from daily stressors. Stepping away from stress is important, but doing so in nature is even more beneficial. Environmental scientists have tried to identify why nature is so therapeutic. One factor they have identified is "instinctual fascination," which happens whenever we are in natural environments.[3] This instinctual fascination is awe and wonder! As Bible-believing Christians, we know that God intentionally created the world with the order that we find in creation, and creation is meant to lead to awe and worship of the Creator; nature was created to be restorative because it was created for humanity. Science often reveals what the Bible has pointed out for centuries: God created all of creation to point to Him, the source *and* object of our awe and wonder.

My friend Ginny Yurich, author, speaker, and founder of 1000 Hours Outside, encourages families to set a goal to spend one thousand hours in the outdoors each year. She inspires families to embrace the gift of wonder by enjoying more time outside. What started as a little experiment with her young family grew into a nationwide phenomenon with over five hundred thousand families joining her! These families are reaping the benefits of prioritizing time outside.

Paul David Tripp says it best:

God created an awesome world. God intentionally loaded the world with amazing things to leave you astounded. The carefully air-conditioned termite mound in Africa, the tart crunchiness of an apple, the explosion of thunder, the beauty of an orchid, the inter-dependent systems of the human body, the inexhaustible pounding of the ocean waves, and thousands of other created sights, sounds, touches, and tastes—God designed all to be awesome. And he intended you to be daily amazed.[4]

This is the essence of wonder. It does not have to only be induced by creation; wonder can come from ideas and new experiences too. Wonder stimulates our minds to think deeply about things, to contemplate, to question. Armstrong wrote, "learning experiences that have the greatest impact on students are often those that involve awe or wonder."[5] This means that when we experience awe, we are hardwired by God to retain and remember; we are primed to learn. Like so many of the qualities we will talk about in this book, it is amazing how God created our minds to process these qualities with a built-in reward system for our brains to want to experience more of it.

Can you think of examples of this in your children's life? I know I can! The times I have been most passionate about a topic always began with amazement and wondering more about it. In college, I knew early on that I wanted to study psychology, specifically a child's brain and behavior development. I was fascinated by how our brains grow, learn, and adapt. I remember sitting in the classroom and learning about the intricate details of the brain and the way that different areas control many different behaviors. I was in awe of how God created our brains to learn languages and complex emotions. It was this awe that drove me to learn more. If I had simply memorized facts for a test, I wouldn't have truly learned anything, but because I was fascinated with the topic, I wanted to learn all I could. I read about the child's developing brain and the way an infant's tiny brain starts out with only 2,500 synapses per neuron; yet by age two or three, the brain has developed roughly 15,000 per neuron! Those synapses are responsible for the explosive learning that takes place during the early years, and any damage or delay in brain development leads to significant long-term developmental delays.[6] I probably bored my roommates to death with all the information I wanted to share.

This is exactly what wonder creates—a desire to know even more. I bet you can think of a time when that's been true for your child too. Do your kids think deeply about something and then want to tell you all about it?

My son was notorious for this right around bedtime. He would ask me the deepest, most spiritual questions. I was always amazed at how his mind worked as he went on to explain what made him make those connections. One night, after I'd tucked him into bed and we'd said our nightly prayers, he asked a question: Since the people of faith in the Old Testament died before Jesus was born, would they still go to heaven? Even if I wasn't always a fan of his timing—I was ready to head to bed myself—I appreciated how he wondered about big things. I answered his question like I oftentimes do, first telling him what a great question that was. And while I know that the people of faith in the Old Testament would be in heaven, I wasn't exactly sure how to explain that in relation to Scripture, so I told him we'd ask our pastor and see what we could find out together.

I've always encouraged him to keep thinking deeply, to ask questions, to search out the answers because this is where wonder is ignited; this is where we develop the skills in life that help us to become the people God created us to be. We will talk even more about curiosity and the many, many questions our kids ask us (and why that's a good thing), but for now I want you to think about how we encourage our kids to stop and think, to wonder about things.

Why don't we naturally experience wonder all day long?

One reason we do not experience wonder more regularly is because we don't slow down long enough to usher it in. One of the culprits that steals our time will come as no surprise—it is the overuse, and abuse, of technology. We all know how dependent, and yes, addicted we are to our phones. I know I am guilty of using my phone to check out, and a few minutes of scrolling somehow becomes an hour. Even as I am writing this book, I find my phone to be a distraction. Thankfully, I have discovered the "do not disturb" mode and it has helped quiet the constant notifications.

Technology not only fuels the lie that we are the center of our universe, it steals our face-to-face connection. Isolating our children from human interaction leads to more self-focus, entitlement, and overstimulation. Dr. Kathy writes that "the human heart will always long for the deeper connection of person-to-person."[7]

Is this a problem in your home? I know for our family we are constantly in the battle against technology addiction. It isn't until we stop making time to do the things we know are important, like family game night or movie night, that I begin to notice that bad habits have snuck back in. Technology is a thief of quality time.

Even the famous movie director Steven Spielberg recognizes the potential for technology to prevent us from having time to ponder as "it interrupts . . . our ability to have a thought or a daydream, to imagine something wonderful because we are too busy bridging the walk from the cafeteria to the office on the cell phone."[8] Now I know this isn't an easy battle to fight. Most of us can't ban all electronic devices from our homes. But we can set ourselves and our families up to be better equipped for the battle. We can set timers, decide as a family what healthy technology use looks like, and even draw up technology "contracts," spelling out the boundaries and consequences around tech use. It is easy to feel overwhelmed in this struggle, but there is hope! The first step is recognizing the problem and deciding to do things differently. You must firmly believe that the convenience of technology is not worth losing valuable time connecting as a family. Remember, to make room for wonder, we must have time to slow down.

Technology is not the only time-sucking culprit. Another is our culture's insistence that fast-paced, jam-packed schedules will help us achieve optimal productivity, that we have no time to slow down and notice the world, let alone experience awe. Do you struggle with a busy schedule and no downtime? I challenge you to ask yourself this: "Do we allow our children time to sit in quiet and observe, think, and ponder? Are we so busy rushing from one activity to the next that we miss out on those important slow times?"

Families today are in danger of living as if more is better—the lie that if we are sitting still, we are not being productive. And productivity and multitasking are supposed to be hallmarks of success. Behavioral scientists looking at productivity are finding what God's Word has been telling us all along[9]—being still and slowing down is good for us. Psalm 37:7 tells us to "be still before the LORD and wait patiently for him" (ESV), and Psalm 46:10 tells us to "be still, and know that I am God" (ESV). Being still is a command from God. Jesus modeled this for us as well. Throughout the Gospels, we see Jesus getting away from the crowds, going to a secluded place to be alone.[10] The brain is a powerful engine, capable of amazing feats, but it needs downtime to recharge. Johns Hopkins, a top ranked children's hospital, educates parents about the danger of keeping children so busy. They describe anxiety, depression, physical symptoms like headaches and stomachaches, as well as poor performance in school, as symptoms of overscheduled kids.[11] We know we need to do something about this; we know we need to slow down and recharge, but we still struggle!

As with technology, combating this begins with awareness. We can't stop there, we must intentionally set boundaries for our children, careful not to overschedule. It is our responsibility to heed the warning signs and stop the frantic pace in order to give ourselves and our children the vital time to be still, to ponder, to be in awe of something, and to take the focus off ourselves and open our eyes to the big, beautiful world around us. Our children need time to recharge!

Ways to encourage wonder in our children

If recharging is important for wonder, then what does that look like?

For my husband, John, his downtime is often talking or processing out loud, but he still needs times of peace, calm, and rest. For me, recharging is found in quiet, in solitude. Going for a run outside in nature is where I can best think and ponder. Neither way is the "right" way to recharge. God created each of us uniquely, with different needs, just like He created each of my children, and yours, uniquely. We must know ourselves, and we must know our children, so we will be able to identify the best ways to set aside time for recharging.

Be intentional about what activities you choose to say yes to and decide as a family what slowing down will look like. Jesus modeled this rhythm of rest. His time of ministry was filled with amazing miracles and a lot of traveling, yet He took time to rest. He would go away to be alone with the Father.[12] He would make time to sleep.[13] And He took time away from the crowds.[14] If Jesus needed times of rest, then how much more do our children? I think we all can agree that our kids need good sleep. They also need time for mental and emotional rest, time to be alone with their thoughts, and if they are Christians then they need spiritual rest during quiet time with the Lord. Again, these times of rest may look different for each child; one may enjoy quietly coloring while another may find that soft music helps to quiet themselves. When we can recharge and rest, we are primed and ready to spark wonder.

Another great way to allow for wonder to develop in our kids and in ourselves is to spend time in nature. Charlotte Mason wrote: "Never be within doors when you can rightly be without."[15] We love to go to our local park. The well-worn paths among the tall Spanish oak trees make the perfect place to observe nature. Sometimes we head into the woods on the lookout for the butterflies in migration. We count how many we can spot and investigate the ones that have made their way closer to our path. Other times we simply show up in the woods, no agenda or purpose, aside from being outside. We always find something that draws our attention— a rotted tree stump with freshly sprouted mushrooms or a pair of squirrels chasing each other from branch to branch. These observations inevitably lead to questions: *Can we eat the mushrooms?* one child asks. *I wonder how long the mommy squirrel stays with the babies,* another ponders.

Some days I dread packing everyone up for a walk through the park; it can be inconvenient for sure. But I never regret our trips because we always come back feeling refreshed and wondering about something new. How about you? Does your family enjoy nature walks? Do you look for ways to draw your children's attention toward something in creation? If you don't, I challenge you to try it—go for a nature walk. Point out the beauty that is all around. By doing this, we will also be helping our children to realize that there is so much in the world to wonder about. That's where the magic happens. This is the miraculous benefit of slowing down and making time for wonder. We are helping our children to live the abundant life God desires for us all.

Wonder is the key that unlocks the potential for all the other qualities we will talk about next. But without the time to reflect and the desire to know more, none of the other qualities will have the opportunity to take root. This is why wonder is one of the essential building blocks to helping our children become who God created them to be. Wonder is the spark that we all desire for a fulfilling and rich life, and we should want this for our whole family!

The days may be long, but the years truly do fly by. Slowing down to savor it all is not only good role modeling for our children, but as parents, we will collect sweet memories to treasure years down the road. Prioritize taking time today in order to invest in tomorrow.

Chapter 4

Vitality

At times, I have felt as if I've lost my vitality, my spark or zest for life. Recently, in fact, I had been in a rut, stuck in my routine, and honestly overwhelmed with everything going on. Rushing from one activity or responsibility to another and neglecting time to slow down and enjoy life had drained me. I had become so worn down that I was missing the forest for the trees in my life as a mom and wife. We don't realize how important slowing down and getting proper perspective is until that's missing. But once we find it again, once we make time to be still and allow God to remind us how amazing life is, we realize vitality is essential for living the abundant, fulfilling life God intends . . . and I had lost it.

Thankfully, I was blessed to get some time away. I was able to have time in new surroundings, with beautiful views and a little peace and quiet. For me, vitality is found in slowing down, being in nature, marveling at God's creation, being still enough to hear His voice . . . and that is exactly what I was able to find to restore my zest for life. We discussed wonder and how important it is to take time to marvel at creation. For me, and others, this is necessary to experience vitality. If we are hurrying through life not slowing down to notice the beauty around us, we will be lacking in both wonder and vitality, and I would argue we would be living a pretty dull existence. I know I was!

WHAT IS VITALITY?

Vitality is unique to each person; the way we experience and express our zest for life may look different for different people. Defining it is like trying to describe spiciness. For some people, like my children, mild salsa is considered spicy; but for others, jalapeño peppers are not spicy at all. Some people are created with a need for more vitality, whereas others are content with just a little. But what *is* universal is that vitality, "aliveness, spontaneity, or vibrancy,"[1] is essential to an abundant life. Vitality has the root word "vital," meaning essential, and the definition includes the "capacity to live and develop."[2] I would argue vitality is not just a capacity to live but an eagerness toward living.

Most children are born with natural excitement for life. They are ready to explore, savor, and experience their world, and they can't wait to tell you all about it. Children with especially high vitality are excited about everything. Sadly, these children are sometimes labeled "too much" or "a lot" because of their eagerness to take in everything, all the time, sometimes at a breakneck pace that's hard to keep up with. Rather than seeing their energy and zeal as a problem to manage, we should see it as a gift to cultivate, and we can help them thrive and learn how to harness that energy for a good purpose.

Maybe you can relate to this. Do you have a child who is excited about a lot of things, eager to share and explore and describe every detail of an experience? Are they ever told to calm down, to be quiet, or to just stop? My friend's daughter radiates her enthusiasm for life. You can just look at her and see how her face lights as she experiences everything around her. She eagerly chats about her most recent topic of interest with anyone who will listen. Last week her fascination was with mermaids, and she couldn't stop talking about the shimmer of the mermaid's tail and how deep the fictional sea creatures can dive. I'm glad my friend understands that her daughter's delight is a beautiful gift to encourage. Sadly, I also see children who bubble up with eagerness to investigate something new, only to be met with an adult who tells them to stop being annoying. Sometimes its actual words that halt kids in their excitement. Other times, it is our actions, like when we don't stop to pay attention to what they are impassioned to show us.

Let's stop seeing vitality and excitement for life as a luxury or a child-ish thing. Instead, let's view this as a tool that God has placed in each of us—this desire for an abundant life. Christians should be the most eager to live the life God has for them, excited for the adventures that await. Viewing this life with purpose and knowing God is unfolding our stories right before our eyes, we should be eager with anticipation about what is next. What you are excited by? What is God doing in your life that you can share with your children?

If vitality comes from understanding that God has a unique purpose for each of us, then our children's gifts, strengths, and abilities will help them fulfill those unique purposes. Our job is to help our children discover those traits God has given them.

As they discover their purposes and strengths, we can teach and model to our children how to use them for God's glory. In whatever ways God has gifted our children, whether it's in sports, or music, or academics, we want to help them understand where those gifts come from and who should be getting the glory.

Be prepared, because their zeal can sometimes be misplaced. Especially gifted children who are passionate about their gifts but might overlook the Giver of those gifts, leading to unhealthy pride. Other children may become fascinated with a topic that is dangerous for them. A teen who is excited by violent video games, for example, should be educated about the dangers of such passions. While we want our children to find things that excite them, things they are passionate about, we must teach them to think on things that are true and honorable and pure.[3] Our children need to not only know how to discern what is good and right to think on (this is wisdom), they must learn proper time, place, and people with which to share their passions. Imagine a child running up to a pastor mid-eulogy during a funeral, bursting to tell him about the newest video game. We never want to shame our children for not knowing how to properly express their vitality; they are doing what comes naturally. Instead, we want to teach them how to handle their zeal appropriately.

Now I understand the realities of parenting, of managing a household with lots of people and moving parts. If we all were full of vitality and passion all day long, we wouldn't accomplish any tasks, especially the tasks no one wants to do, like laundry and dishes! Can you picture nonstop energy directed toward whatever your child's latest passion might be? Without boundaries and self-discipline, things could get out of hand pretty quickly, right? I am not advocating for that kind of chaos! But there might need to be room for a little chaos from time to time.

In our house, my daughter bursts with excitement over planning parties. Every opportunity she gets, she wants to host a party or event. Recently, she hosted a movie-watching party for her siblings. She printed off movie tickets, planned a menu, and set up a concession stand with snacks. She makes decorations that match the theme of the movie and rearranges the living room to make it more like a theater. She loves the planning, the decorating, the hosting of her siblings. Every time she comes up with a new party idea, she gets excited and energized. I love this about her (and that she gets it from me because I too love a themed party!).

But if I let her run without boundaries, she would never clean up after one party before moving on to the next. She would only eat the snacks that she plans for the parties, and she would never be hungry for dinner. She would never want to do schoolwork, housework, or basically anything that didn't spark her interest. And in her immaturity, she would love to be allowed to live like that all the time. Because I want her to learn the importance of discipline, hard work, and diligence, I do not allow her to jump to another project before finishing the previous one well. She'll learn the balance between play and completing tasks that must be done, and how God desires for us to do both without discouraging her vitality.

This quality of vitality is a beautiful thing and brings abundant life and excitement to the everyday. But as Dr. Kathy says, "Anything well done, overdone, is badly done."[4] And that is so true for any of these traits! Too much of any good thing is not good at all. So, we must teach our children how to use these gifts well, to God's glory and within healthy boundaries. That's true for all of life, right? Chocolate is a wonderful gift from the Lord, but if that's all I ever eat, I will be sorely lacking in nutrition and probably have a terrible stomachache. Some families choose to only have chocolate on special occasions, while others say that a daily treat of chocolate is okay. Each family is unique. Each family gets to decide what boundaries are good for them.

Your family may be more structured and function best on routine and schedule. If that is you, vitality may look different in your home. Other families may be more free-spirited and laid back on the routines and schedules. Vitality will be expressed differently for them, but we all can find reasons to live each day with eager anticipation for what God has in store.

If vitality is so good for us, why can we seem to lose it?

Many of us get so busy in our day-to-day lives that we don't take time to slow down. We talked about the importance of doing just that, being still, and giving ourselves margin to rest. You will notice the theme of rest in almost every chapter because in order to activate these qualities in our homes and in our children, time is required. And time is not something we just find; we must carve it out and protect it.

Besides making time to slow down, a lot of us shift into autopilot in our lives. We go through the motions, checking off the boxes so we can move on to the next thing. But we can miss the wonder of creation; we can miss questions from and conversations with our children; and we can miss seeing God's hand at work in our lives. What priorities are we demonstrating based on how we spend our time? Do we wake up excited to live the abundant life God has called us to? If not, how can we see life as an exciting story we get to be a part of instead of just another day to endure?

Ways to invite vitality into your home

Vitality is a key that unlocks the abundant life God created. It is important to learning, to parenting, and to our family's overall well-being. Now let's look at some practical ways to encourage this quality to flourish.

Practice using all five senses. This may seem silly at first, especially with older children, but by tuning in to all our senses, we notice things we may not normally pay attention to. You can tell your child to freeze and ask them: What do you see, what do you hear, what do you feel, what do you taste, what do you smell? As they practice noticing their senses, they may begin to do it without your prompting. Make sure to celebrate the things they notice. This activity is also a wonderful opportunity to talk about how amazing it is that God created them with senses so that they can smell the brownies baking for dessert or see their dog's tail wagging because *he's* happy to see *them*!

Play games that involve noticing details. We like to play "I Spy," the game where you "spy" something around you that is a certain color and then everyone else tries to figure out what you are "spying." This gets children to pay attention to details around them. You may be surprised at the things they notice. Again, the more we celebrate the things they notice the more likely they are to continue to pay attention to details around them. The goal is to celebrate the world around us and tune in to things. The more we are able to tune in to the world the more we will experience the world around us!

Set aside time to note the little joys of the day. Mealtime is a great opportunity for each person to share a highlight from their day. At first, if your family isn't naturally tuned in to these details, this may take some effort. But by modeling this practice of sharing details of our own day, we will teach our children to pay attention and be ready to have something exciting to share. During our mealtimes, we each take turns sharing the highlight of our day. Sometimes these conversations are short and sweet; other times they become longer talks.

Expect the unexpected. One of my favorite ways to encourage vitality in our home is a trick I learned from author Julie Bogart in her book *The Brave Learner*. She talks about "the magic of surprise."[5] By sprinkling unexpected things into our daily routine, we catch our children off guard and often spark vitality. I do this during our homeschool day. I will surprise the kids with a walk to the park or a tea party. I've even come to the table wearing a tiara! These unexpected moments bring excitement and joy into our homes and break us out of our ruts. This doesn't always have to involve big things. Just an unexpected hug or tickle is enough to invite some vitality into our day. One day, I surprised our youngest, Charlotte, with a Silly String fight. She was so excited to actually be allowed to cover Mom with long strands of gooey pink string. It brought a spark to both our days!

New experiences are an easy way to usher vitality into a family. As I mentioned in the chapter on wonder, we love to travel and explore new places. Many of the twelve qualities are awakened when we encounter new experiences. Vitality is especially awakened when our senses are tuned in to locations, interactions, and activities that are unfamiliar. Traveling to a different city is great, but adventure can also be found right outside your front door. My daughters are adept at encouraging me to go on adventures with them. There are days when I just don't feel like leaving the house. When I remember how important it is to get outside and break up our routine, I will say yes. Adventure may be inconvenient, but the impact can be lifelong.

When we remember the big picture purpose of parenting—to help our children become who God has uniquely created them to be—it is much easier to eagerly anticipate each adventure that lies before us. When we parent with the end in mind, it makes all the sacrifice and inconvenience not seem so difficult. An essential part of remembering the big picture is taking time to slow down, be still, and let God remind us of who He is and what He enables us to do. This is a surefire way to keep the spark alive in our families and in our homes.

Chapter 5

Sensitivity

I was born one of those deep-feeling, sensitive types. As far back as I can remember, I have felt things acutely. I have always been the friend who attracts others with deep pains or trauma. Through this gift, the Lord allows me to comfort and encourage them. God created me with this natural desire to tune in to other people's feelings and circumstances, and it was this drive that led me to a degree in mental health counseling.

Human connection is rooted in emotional connection. And we are created to thrive with healthy human connections. Children who lack this basic human need of emotional connection suffer devastating, long-lasting trauma. Armstrong defines sensitivity as an openness to the world around us.[1] It is essential to emotional connection to others. Sensitivity creates caring and compassionate people, something we need more of in this world. It is the caring and compassionate people who see a problem and are moved to do something about it.

But I remember a time when I did not see this quality of sensitivity as a gift; in fact, I hated that I was so emotionally tuned in to others.

One day, while in high school youth group, I took a spiritual gifts inventory, an assessment that identifies what type of spiritual gifts have been placed by the Holy Spirit once you accept Christ. Although my results did not surprise me, they were a bit discouraging.

You see, many of my friends ranked high in what I considered "practical" gifts: teaching, hospitality, exhortation, evangelism. Me? I ranked high in mercy. I remember reading those results and feeling so discouraged because to me, the gift of mercy was sort of a useless gift. I believed that having the gift of mercy meant that, while I could cry with someone if they were grieving, I wasn't really helping them. I wanted a gift that provided tangible, immediate results, something a little more showy, I guess. My teenage self had so much to learn!

Thankfully, with maturity and life experience, I have come to value this gift of mercy, this ability to feel others' pain deeply, to join them in their hurt, and to just be present. I cannot count how many times this gift has been used to minister to friends, family, and even strangers.

WHAT IS SENSITIVITY?

Now I want to make a distinction between the spiritual gift of mercy and the quality of sensitivity. The gift of mercy is imparted in believers by the Holy Spirit at salvation. Sensitivity is a quality we are all created with, some to higher degrees than others. For those not naturally high in sensitivity, growth can occur. And if our children are high in sensitivity, they might only experience the overwhelming feelings that can occur, while not understanding that it is a wonderful quality. Our job is to help them see the blessing of sensitivity and grow in areas where they need to grow, while celebrating the quality.

As a young mom, I began to value sensitivity as I taught my children to be aware of others' feelings. I still didn't necessarily value my own sensitivity, but I did understand that I wanted my children to be empathetic to others and be able to articulate what they were feeling, so I could guide them on how to handle those feelings appropriately. Looking back at that season, knowing what I know now, I am so thankful to the Holy Spirit for guiding my parenting and for the education in mental health counseling I was receiving.

Guiding others toward healthy expressions of their emotions was just one of the lessons I was learning, and I wanted to teach these lessons to my children. Through healthy emotions, we can relate best to God and others. I want this for my family, and I want this for myself. And I bet you do too.

During my training, we reviewed many case studies of individuals who had not learned how to express emotions or had unhealthy examples of expressing them. I saw firsthand the dangerous behaviors that occur if we do not teach sensitivity to our children. Not long after I graduated with my master's degree, I got an even clearer picture of what happens when we don't teach our kids empathy and provide a safe environment for developing emotional health.

Fresh out of seminary, my first job as a clinical counselor was working with teenage girls at a juvenile detention facility. During my time with these young women, we talked a lot about emotions, naming them, and learning how to express them in healthy ways.

Every single one of these girls struggled with empathy and compassion, which made it hard for them to understand why destructive, hurtful behaviors were dangerous and wrong. For each of them, the reasons for their incarcerations could be traced back to a lack of emotional regulation or lack of empathy.

In my professional experience, it is much easier to encourage and to teach sensitivity when kids are very young than after the walls are built and they have decided emotions are bad or scary. But it isn't hopeless. Some of these young women grew tremendously during our time together, but it required years of therapy and hard work to build the foundation of emotional health.

I have a daughter who has always experienced emotions on a deeper level than any of her siblings. She is alert to the feelings of those around her, and she is often moved by compassion toward others. Sometimes her big feelings can be overwhelming to her, causing her to shut down or avoid situations where she becomes overstimulated by feelings.

This was most obvious whenever we took her to a movie. While my other children loved going to see whatever animated film was playing, eager to have popcorn and a drink while watching the big screen, she was not a fan . . . at all. As young as the age of two or three, I remember her crying (screaming) and begging us not to make her go into the theater. She did not have the vocabulary then to tell us that it was too loud and too dark and the movies made her feel overwhelmed, but she sure told us in her own way.

The first several times we tried to go to the movies as a family, either John or I would spend the majority of the film holding her right outside the theater doors. We hoped she would outgrow this fear of movie theaters, but eventually we realized that this was just not something she was going to enjoy at this stage. So, as a family we adjusted, and we planned movie trips whenever she would be at a friend's house. As she matured, she was able to explain that the bigness of the screen amplified the bigness of her empathy. When a character on screen, even an animated one, hurt or was afraid, she felt those feelings in extreme ways. She just didn't know how to handle all those huge feelings projected in widescreen.

She didn't become the center of the household, dictating what we were allowed to do. Instead, we talked as a family about the importance of taking one another's feelings into consideration. It would have been easy for the younger sisters to get frustrated and feel that one sibling could ruin this family activity, but because talking about emotions and supporting one another has become the fabric of our home, they are much more understanding. We do not shame anyone for any feeling, and we encourage each other to express how we feel.

Do we still get frustrated sometimes? Absolutely. But those moments offer even more opportunities for us to talk about putting ourselves in the other person's shoes and putting others first. We see how Jesus demonstrated this by laying down His life, and how Paul described considering others as more important than ourselves in his letter to the Philippians.[2] Both are essential skills for empathy!

Now that our sensitive daughter is a teenager, she still doesn't love to go to the movies, but she has learned to adapt so that she can join us occasionally for a family film. We have empowered her to find coping skills that work for her, and it has made a big difference.

I know that we all have times of impatience and lack of compassion when someone's big feelings are inconvenient or even annoying or frustrating. I bet you can think of your own children having hurt feelings and difficult emotions to navigate. Do you take the time to talk about emotions and discuss healthy ways to handle them? Let's strive to make it a priority!

I often find myself struggling with my own feelings and staying calm while helping my family navigate their own emotions. I still catch myself downplaying emotions, stuffing them down instead of bringing them to the Lord or a trusted friend. What about you? I have a suspicion that I am not the only parent who would benefit from some resources and help. I want you to know that it is okay to struggle! We are human and we are growing alongside our families.

What gets in the way of developing sensitivity?

As parents, we cannot teach what we do not possess. I am passionate about the importance of cultivating this God-given quality of sensitivity in ourselves. Mental health impacts every area of our lives, and good mental health must be prioritized—in us, in our families, and in our children.

Maybe you are reading this and realize that you or a family member has experienced trauma, difficulties, or unhealthy ways of coping. Do you need help addressing this? I urge you to seek help. If your child had an injury or disease, you would find a doctor who could provide healing treatment. In the same way, if you or your child is struggling with trauma, anxiety, depressive thoughts, or difficulty coping, the very best thing you can do for your family is to seek professional help.

Growing emotionally healthy and mature is a journey. None of us is ever finished learning and growing. In our family, we work hard to give our children the vocabulary to identify feelings. We work on providing the space to express those feelings and validate emotions as good gifts from God, but we still struggle to express our feelings in the healthiest way.

As the mom to teenagers, I am learning how to parent in the midst of all the emotional roller coasters that come with this season of life. And I will keep doing the same things I did when I first started out as a brand-new mom; I'm praying for God's leading, and I'm seeking out people smarter and more experienced along the way who can offer wisdom and guidance. Keep asking insightful questions and give space for thoughtful conversations, because this is essential in boosting sensitivity and emotional wholeness.

Are you ready to be intentional about making space for sensitivity in your home? I'm going to give you some practical ideas for how to do this—how to ask good questions, how to recognize unhealthy emotions, and how to spot a few warning signs—so you can empower *your* kids to express their feelings in healthy ways.

Human connection and secure attachments are the foundation from which our children grow and thrive. Always remember this: your relationship with your child is the most important thing—more important than their obedience or intelligence, definitely more important than a clean house or looking like the perfect family. A strong relationship is foundational to helping our children become who God created them to be. "For your children to want what you want for them, for changes to occur, and for improvements to remain, your hearts must be inter-twined,"[3] writes Dr. Kathy. God designed the family, the home, to be the foundation where our children's view of God and His faithfulness grow. It is within the relationships at home that our children learn how to relate to others and to God.

But relationships can feel inconvenient sometimes. They take time and investment, and require putting others' needs before our own. Any sacrifice we make in order to prioritize healthy relationships is always, always, worth it. The long-term gain is far greater than any loss! And as we make this investment, we may realize it is not all that bothersome after all, but an honor and privilege.

How can we help our children grow in openness to the world around them?

One important way to encourage sensitivity is through engaging conversations with our children. We must be aware of nonverbal cues, facial expressions, body language, and eye contact. Are we distracted by our phones? (I'm talking to myself on this one too!) Are we looking them in the eye and nodding our heads as our kids talk? Doing this communicates that we're listening to them. Are we asking good open-ended questions and allowing them time to answer? Are we genuinely interested in what they say to us? Or do we dismiss what they say as unimportant? All of this sends the message to our children that what they say matters. If they believe we want to hear what they say, they will be much more likely to keep communication open. And open commu-nication is essential to a healthy relationship.

We must also pay attention to *their* nonverbal cues. Observe them. Study their facial expressions. We parents know our kids best. When we take time, we will notice when they are struggling emotionally. Some of those behavioral clues to watch out for include:

- any dramatic changes to their personality or behavior
- prolonged sadness that does not seem to get better after a few weeks
- increased withdrawing
- other more obvious signs like self-harm

If you see any of these behaviors in your child, then you need to seek professional intervention. But often, the behaviors we may notice will not be as severe, and addressing emotional needs before they become extreme can help stop a negative spiral. As Christian parents, we have the added benefit of the Holy Spirit to assist us with discerning deeper issues.

And then we help them label those emotions that they may not realize they are experiencing. With little ones, this may simply mean naming out loud the emotion they are expressing. For example, I could say, "Charlotte, it looks like you are angry because your sister took your toy. Do you feel angry?" By observing how she is feeling and helping her label that feeling, she will be better equipped to recognize that emotion the next time.

But we don't just want to name the emotion. We must validate their feelings while also guiding them on how to express that emotion in a healthy way. It might look like saying, "Charlotte, I bet you are angry because she took your toy. I would be angry too. But remember, we can't let our anger cause us to hurt someone else. That's sin. You can tell your sister that she made you mad when she took your toy and then ask for it back."

Have you had that conversation in your home? It's not usually neat and tidy, with the offending child giving the toy right back. Practicing the response lays the groundwork for helping our children express emotions, understand empathy, and grow in their sensitivity toward others.

By normalizing emotions, we help our children understand that feelings are healthy; they are tools God gives us to relate to others. Our job is to teach them how to express those emotions in healthy ways. Typically, children will stuff their feelings down, withdraw, deny, or explode. These are not healthy ways of expressing emotions. We must teach them, instead, how to identify, process, and express their feelings in safe, God-honoring ways. Sometimes it is hard to find a healthy expression for emotions, especially for children as they grow older and their emotions become more complicated. But what has always been true is that we human beings are meant to express our emotions, to share them with someone else. And parents should be the safe place for children to go to with all their emotions.

One tool we use in our home is a feelings journal, where my daughters can write down anything that they are feeling. Writing them down can be easier than saying our thoughts and emotions out loud in front of someone. Another technique I use in counseling is to engage in a small activity while sitting beside the person who is sharing. Being side by side makes opening up about feelings much less threatening than when sitting face to face, staring into each others' eyes. Boys, especially, open up more when they are busy doing something with their hands. So, the next time you want your child to share how they are feeling, try going for a walk or coloring next to one another. See if this posture makes sharing a little less awkward.

While teaching our children to express emotions is important, we must teach them that we aren't controlled by our emotions, either. Author Lysa TerKeurst explains that our feelings don't tell us what to do, they simply inform of us what is going on under the surface.[4] Children need to understand that feelings can tell us what's going on inside of us (again, they can be tools from the Lord), but they are not always true. The prophet Jeremiah warned, "The heart is more deceitful than all else and is desperately sick; who can understand it?"[5]

In emotionally healthy people, the goal then is to be aware of our emotions and understand how to manage them in productive ways. This is a journey that we will all learn and grow in along the way, but the first step begins at home. Parents have the privilege of setting the foundation of sensitivity, compassion, and emotional health. We get the honor of creating safe, healthy, secure attachments with our children that set them up for future success in relationships and life.

Whole books have been written on this topic of emotional health and wholeness. It is a topic I'm passionate about and could probably keep writing about for many more pages. But the main takeaway is that we are all created with an openness to the world around us. And our job as parents is to continue to encourage this quality in ourselves and in our families so that our children can become the caring, compassionate people God created them to be. And when trauma or mental illness threaten to close us or our children off to the gift of sensitivity, I pray that we have the wisdom to seek the help we need to heal.

Chapter 6

Flexibility

Have you ever had a conversation where the person jumps from one topic to another? To you, the topics seem to have nothing to do with each other, and you struggle to keep up with their drastic changes in topics. This is most conversations with my husband, John. He starts out talking about a phone call that he just finished, filling me in on more details than I need. Then he shifts gears and reminds me that the car is due for an oil change, next reminding me that he is planning on flying out of town next Monday. Then he shares about a family vacation that he has in mind and asks when I think we can schedule a week of family time. How his mind goes from a phone call, to an oil change, to his travel schedule, to family vacation I can't fully understand. If you ask him, however, he can tell you exactly how each topic is connected in his flexible mind. After being married to him for almost twenty years, I have learned how quickly and fluidly his mind works. To a casual observer, his thoughts may look like unconnected pieces of a puzzle, but to John, and others like him, the connections are obvious. This is what makes John so ingenious! He can envision how all the pieces fit before the big picture even comes together. This makes him a brilliant strategist. He sees connections between ideas and information that others miss entirely. He is extremely gifted in flexibility.

WHAT IS FLEXIBILITY?

When you hear "flexibility," you may picture super bendy people who can touch their toes. It reminds me of the Presidential Fitness Challenge of my school years. The "sit and stretch" was probably the only event where I actually met the standards. I could never do the rope climb or run the mile fast enough, but I could always count on being able to pull off sitting on the ground and touching my toes. Clearly, I wasn't the most athletic student, but I was pretty flexible. This, however, is not the type of flexibility I am talking about. Instead, I'm talking about mental flexibility.

This is the ability to make connections between seemingly unrelated topics.[1] Armstrong emphasizes the child's ability to move from fantasy to reality and back as the main feature of flexible thinking. And while I agree that is part of it, I also believe it encompasses a mind that can stretch and adapt new information. Flexible thinkers are great problemsolvers. Much like creativity and inventiveness, which we will discuss in later chapters, this quality allows us to be open and receptive to new ideas and information. A buzzword in education circles is "growth mindset." Carol Dwek was the first to report research on growth mindset in students in 2006. She defined it as a student's belief that they are capable of growing in their knowledge and ability, that learning was not fixed but could grow.[2]

Much more research has been done since Dwek's work in 2006, and findings suggest that children with a positive growth mindset are better equipped to handle setbacks, deal with uncertainty, and learn new skills and understand new ideas more easily.[3] Rigid thinkers lack this flexibility when faced with setbacks or things not going their way. Much like a brittle rubber band when pulled taut, rigid thinkers snap when put under the pressure of new information that doesn't fit into their preconceived ideas. They are unable to consider any other viewpoint and are unable to change their minds about situations regardless of new facts presented. Can you picture someone like that? Perhaps one of your children loses it when things don't go their way.

In contrast, flexible thinkers who hold ideas with humility can adapt to new ideas and information without breaking. Flexible thinkers realize that new ideas and information may be added to what they already know and are able to expand and change their understanding given new information. This doesn't mean that flexible thinkers do not hold firm to beliefs, like a biblical worldview. But it does mean that they are able to view information from others' perspectives and have civil discussions around ideas—even ideas with which they strongly disagree—without feeling threatened. In today's culture, we need more people able to have civil discourse without snapping.

And the good news is our children start out with flexible thinking— some of us more than others, like John who is very gifted in this area. Young children are learning what information to filter out and what is most important, so nothing seems absurd or unreasonable—all information is considered important and relevant. As human beings mature and our brains learn to filter out unnecessary information, our flexible thinking becomes more fixed. Some of this is necessary for our brains to make quicker connections between the thousands of neurons firing all at once. We pull from previous experience in order to know what to expect in new situations. But sometimes the information we filter out can actually be helpful.

There have been a few fascinating studies that demonstrate that expertise doesn't always increase performance. One study looked at how the presence of an attending physician impacted medical errors and patient safety compared to when residents cared for patients on their own, without the senior attending physician present. This study found no statistical difference between the presence or absence of the attending doctor.[4] It is initially surprising because you would assume patient care would improve with the most experienced doctor overseeing care. However, some suggest that the less experienced student doctors were rigorous in their investigation of symptoms and did not disregard any information as unimportant, like the more seasoned doctors may have, and therefore found more accurate diagnosis and treatments.[5]

It's also good to know that the mortality rate overall is lower at teaching hospitals.[6] This suggests that those who are constantly growing in knowledge and expanding their understanding have better outcomes than those who are not in a learning environment. Our brains are powerful and efficient. God created them that way. We learn behaviors and repeat them often without thinking, but sometimes fixed thinking prevents us from gaining an accurate or more robust understanding.

Think about a behavior that you can do with your eyes closed. We can operate on autopilot pretty easily, right? If we unlock our car the same way each time, we don't even have to think about how to do it. We have an old SUV that still uses a key in the ignition. But when I drive my husband's car, which uses a start button, I still try to insert my key into the ignition because that's my muscle memory. Again, muscle memory helps with efficiency, and that's not a bad thing. But when efficiency comes at the expense of accuracy, like the example with the doctors, it can become problematic!

Flexibility may look like a child who gets easily distracted, noticing something that reminds him of something else he's learned before, and suddenly has questions that may seem irrelevant at the time. Much like his father, our son, Joey, did this when he was in the fourth grade. He was constantly interrupting his teacher with questions and ideas or jumping down rabbit trails as one subject connected to another. For instance, he would hear a story in English class that reminded him of an event in the Bible that triggered a thought about a fact he learned in science. To the teachers, he may have seemed to be "off track," but to his flexible, always agile mind, these connections were perfectly clear.

This is one of the reasons we decided to homeschool, so our children could go down rabbit trails and explore new connections between subjects. It could be easy to get frustrated with a child like this. The traditional education system is typically set up so that children learn in a linear fashion, one idea or subject at a time and each subject progresses over time. Subjects are "siloed," and rarely do classes consider how subjects intersect with one another. In the last one hundred years, educators have considered the idea of studying subjects more interdependently.

School districts across the United States are adopting this approach to education because it works. Educational researchers looked at results of an interdisciplinary education and found "improved written and oral communication skills, teamwork skills, ethical decision-making, critical thinking, and the ability to apply knowledge in real-world settings—are the very same outcomes that employers and university administrators alike agree students should possess upon graduation."[7] Flexible thinking, pointing out connections, and adapting to new information on a regular basis helps students succeed in school and in life.

A barrier to flexible thinking—fixed or rigid thinking

Children who have rigid thinking not only struggle with a change of plans or new routines, but they also have a harder time with idioms and puns. Sometimes children on the autism spectrum, as well as those with specific learning disabilities, have literal and fixed ways of looking at things. This literal, rigid thinking can lead to difficulties in reading, math, and problem-solving and can cause challenges with social interactions. Teaching these children how to be more flexible and adaptable is typically one part of treatment and intervention. Mixing up a routine, such as sitting in a new spot in the classroom or studying subjects in a new order are small ways to stretch the muscles of flexibility. Even neurotypical children (those who are not on the autism spectrum or don't have a specified learning disability) can still struggle with rigid thinking and getting stuck in a routine.

One of my daughters in particular struggles with flexible thinking. When we have a plan for the day, in her mind it is set and unchanging. When plans change, she becomes unhappy. And with a household of six and a mom and dad in ministry, plans change often. She does not see any room for changes to the plans. Maybe you have a child like this too. Here's an approach we've found helpful that may also help you and your child.

First, acknowledge how frustrating or disappointing it is when plans change. We want to normalize our child's feelings but also teach them healthy ways to cope with those feelings. As mentioned in the chapter on sensitivity, we cannot just expect children to know how to process their feelings, so we need to teach them through discussion and modeling it ourselves. But we don't just stop there. Next, we need to help them come up with solutions on how to overcome the disappointment.

Imagine if you had plans to go over to your child's friend's house for lunch and then to the park. What happens if the friend became ill and the plans change? A child lacking flexibility would be upset and struggle to get over the disappointment of not seeing this friend. In this situation, you start with letting them talk about how they are feeling and why. Ask them to help you come up with a new plan for the day. Brainstorm possible things you could do instead. Perhaps you could tell your child that you will reschedule with their friend for another day. You could suggest making a card and dropping off flowers to the sick friend's front door. I wish I could say that it would be easy to get a child's rigid thinking to become more flexible. It will not. But eventually, with intentional work on your part, they will adjust to the new plan and learn to not let the disappointment totally ruin the day.

We don't want to become permissive parents who try to coddle our children into feeling better by bribing them with something else, like a new toy. We do want to allow our children to feel our empathy and know that we care whenever they are disappointed. We must help equip them to handle disappointments with flexibility because, as we all know, they will continue to experience disappointments.

Do you like the idea of encouraging more flexible thinking in your children? Do you see the benefits, not only for their education but for their future? If so, there are things we can do to bring more flexible thinking into our homes.

Ways to encourage flexibility

One way of encouraging flexible thinking is to give our children plenty of exposure to various concepts and novel experiences that change up the routine to strengthen the muscles of adaptability. Let's demonstrate for our children what flexible thinking looks like. When we choose to be adaptable to new or changing circumstances, they witness firsthand the skills they need to adapt. Say out loud the steps you are taking to solve a problem. Vocalizing your thoughts helps bring your children into the process, showing them how you are flexible in your thinking. Let them hear your feelings when plans change and model for them how maturity responds to those inconveniences.

Allow your children to handle difficult circumstances on their own. We cannot, nor should we, fix all their problems. They must learn the skills to problem-solve. Don't shelter your family from difficulty. Instead, walk alongside them, talking them through how to work out their own struggles. We can cheer them on and assure them that we believe that they are capable of figuring it out. This confidence from Mom and Dad is a big boost for them! If we believe in them, then they are much more likely to believe in themselves. But if we jump in and try to solve it all for them, they will internalize the message that they are not capable of handling things themselves.

Besides allowing our children to overcome big and small obstacles, we can strengthen flexibility by practicing looking at problems in multiple ways, perhaps with different solutions. Through discussion and real-time application, we can teach our children that there is more than one way to solve a problem. Sometimes that can mean setting up a "barrier" to solve as a game to play.

For example, I could call everyone into the kitchen and tell them, "I haven't gone to the store and it's almost dinnertime. We only have these four ingredients. What can we possibly make for dinner?" By allowing the children to search online for recipes, pull out cookbooks, and brainstorm possible meals that could be made with those ingredients, together they figure out a way to solve our dinner dilemma. This is a simple example, but it demonstrates how there are multiple ways to use these different ingredients to prepare a meal for everyone. The family could even choose a "winner" for the most out-of-the-box idea. This not only strengthens flexible thinking, it makes dinner fun! Get your family thinking in new ways and seeing possibilities where they might not have seen them before. At first, they may need some prompting, but with enough practice, they will be solving problems you didn't even know you had. We will talk more about that in the chapter on inventiveness; for now, just know that flexible thinking leads to some pretty incredible inventions!

And just like flexibility can lead to inventiveness, vitality leads to flexibility. Because getting out of ruts helps foster the important gift of vitality, it also leads to new ways of looking at things. Each of these qualities encourages, supports, and blends into one another. You will find as we go along that one small change can have a huge impact. And stretching our family's adaptability is one of those impactful changes!

Another way we can enhance flexible thinking in our homes is to play games that encourage creative thinking. Knowing your child and their unique interests, you can choose games that would appeal to them. I have a few "word smart" kids (one of the "smarts" Dr. Kathy identifies in her book *8 Great Smarts*[8]) who love to play word games. A great game that encourages flexible thinking is Scattergories. In this game, you come up with original words, beginning with the letter that was rolled, for different categories. The more original and creative the word, the more likely you are to get credit for a word that no one else writes down. Get creative by encouraging your children to expand their minds and see things in new ways.

And finally, listen to your children and make time for great discussions. Read books together, watch movies, and discuss the various viewpoints of the characters. Talk about ways the characters could have solved problems differently. Try seeing things from someone else's viewpoint, maybe even someone you disagree with, in order to strengthen the flexibility muscles. Ask questions like "why do you think that character made those decisions?" Remember, we want our children to become adults who can have civil discussions about topics with people, no matter whether they agree or disagree. We want to help our children become those flexible rubber bands that don't snap under pressure but can adapt. I am not saying we want to raise children who don't take a stand or don't believe in firm truth, but we do want to raise children who think well about issues . . . or what Proverbs 15:28 describes as one who "ponders how to answer" instead of the one who "pours out evil."

This gift of flexible thinking has been such a blessing for our family. Because of my husband John's keen mind and ability to see how seemingly unrelated things connect, he has helped businesses grow and thrive and has provided a wonderful life for our family. He can anticipate roadblocks to an organization's success while simultaneously laying out a strategy to circumvent those roadblocks. John's flexible thinking is what makes him such a great visionary and strategist. His ability to think on all available information while simultaneously seeing possibilities where others cannot makes him such an innovative and brilliant businessman.

Flexible thinking can lead to more ideas and questions that develop from considering information in new ways; it's a natural progression. Flexible thinking goes hand in hand with curiosity, as well as inventiveness and creativity. Isn't it amazing how our Creator God designed our minds to work and that each of these qualities flows into one another? They are not exactly linear on a flowchart but more like several tributaries forming a great river. For this river to be its most powerful, each tributary must be strengthened. Awakening one of these qualities will only enhance the others. For example, flexible thinking allows our children to examine all information, not just what everyone else thinks is important, which can lead to curiosity. And curiosity can enhance open-mindedness, which then supports flexible thinking. Let's look for ways to ignite flexibility in our children and see what other qualities show up!

Chapter 7

Curiosity

If you look at any infant, across culture and time, you see an innate drive to explore, to question, to ponder. Infants may not have the vocabulary to ask questions about the world, but their wide eyes and exploring hands, feet, and mouths are constantly searching for answers. *What is that? What does this do? How does this taste?* They point at objects as their way of asking questions. They bang things together to learn cause and effect. They taste to discover. It's just how we are created to be! As parents, we can encourage this natural curiosity, and we want this for our children because curiosity is the root of all learning. Learning is how we become the people God created us to be.

WHAT IS CURIOSITY?

If you've spent any time around children, you know that this curiosity is always bubbling up. It is in elementary-age students when the questions really begin in earnest. Children at this stage of development have the language skills and just enough information about the world to iden- tify and become interested in all sorts of things. They are attempting to make sense of the world around them in concrete ways. Through learning the names of objects and exploring the characteristics of those objects, they are full of questions about everything. Children ask more than one hundred questions per hour on average. The more curious they are, the more questions they ask.[1] And, children ask some of the *best* questions. Our willingness to allow space and freedom for them to ask questions will only encourage them to keep asking even more. The good news is, we don't have to have all the answers. "Even when you don't know the answer, you're letting them know it's good to wonder and ask,"[2] according to beloved children's television host Fred Rogers. "When kids wonder, they are learning—or at least they're far more likely to."[3]

Curiosity, this desire to identify and comprehend more about the world, is a tool that helps our children discover their interests, passions, and possibly their careers. Our job is to encourage our children to keep asking questions, especially as they get older. And as loving parents, we are uniquely poised to meet this special need, and we can provide a safe place for them to ask questions, exactly the way God intended. This is God's intention for your home and for mine. The core need for security is one that God intended to be met first in our homes and ultimately in Him. Security in your relationship with your child is essential in encouraging your child's curiosity to find its answers in you, in wise coun- selors, and in God and His Word. It doesn't matter how educated we are or whether we answer their questions perfectly; our responsibility is to provide a loving, safe home where children will feel secure enough to risk asking and exploring. As children mature into middle and high school students—the questions don't stop. Unfortunately, sometimes where they go to answer those questions becomes problematic. When their only source for answers was Mom and Dad, children had little choice, but as they grow in independence, their access to less reliable sources of information increases. Friends, social media, and Google begin replacing Mom and Dad if questions are squashed at home.

The teen years are arguably the most important time for our children to have a safe and loving place to come with all their questions. Most parents would agree that we want them to see us as their main source of information, but if we have spent the past thirteen years discouraging their curiosity by not providing a space for questioning or allowing them to see us as a reliable source of information, then they will probably stop coming to us altogether.

Tweens and teens start relying on their peers, as well as the internet, to answer their many questions—what a scary thought that is! Rather than talking with parents, teens are often seeking out information from other teens, and together they decide what conclusion to draw from one another. These sources may not be providing biblical information. It is vital that parents make sure their children know that *they* are a reliable place to come to with any and all of their questions.

My children have always had so many questions! They would pepper me with questions, like why is two times two four, why is the sky blue, why does paint turn green when you mix blue and yellow? Sometimes I have a hard time answering the questions that pop up, especially the ones that inevitably come right at bedtime when I have already checked out for the day. Wow, is it inconvenient to take the time to listen. I try to answer with something like, "That's a great question. Let's talk about this first thing tomorrow!"

Have you ever had those right-before-bedtime questions from your child? You can probably think of lots of examples. Whatever the question may be, our response will help determine if our children continue to remain curious.

Validate your child's curiosity. Tell them how great it is to ask questions, and then respond honestly. If you don't know the answer, explain that you could ask someone who might help find the answers. Another skill to model is knowing *who* to ask when we don't have answers.

As they've grown older, the children's questions have become even harder—and sometimes uncomfortable—to answer. I definitely don't always have the answers, but I am willing to sit with them in the tension of the unknown as we search for answers together, even if that searching takes us to challenging places and even when it's inconvenient to do so.

One day at the park, one of my children, seemingly out of the blue, asked me how lesbians can have babies. We had been studying reproduction in science recently, and this flexible-thinking child was making connections between what we were learning in biology and what she was noticing in culture. She simply didn't understand, reproductively, how new life could come from two females. We were in the middle of a public park, and I felt my shoulders tense and my pulse quicken as I tried to decide how to best handle this conversation. After a few deep breaths, I affirmed the question, saying that it was a great question. And then I asked, "What made you think about that?" I wanted to validate curiosity and not shame her for wondering about a topic others may consider embarrassing. I told her that I was glad she was willing to come to me with questions, even questions that may seem embarrassing. I told her that I would be happy to talk more about this topic when we were in private because there were other children around, and this was a conversation that parents have with their own children.

Once we got home, I made sure we revisited the conversation, as awkward as it was. I gave her age-appropriate answers, reminding her what we had already learned about reproduction, and gave a succinct explanation of artificial insemination. Not exactly how I saw that day at the park going! I was, however, glad that my children were coming to me with these questions because left to their own curiosities they may have learned something else entirely. Their minds are constantly making sense of the world around them, and it is a beautiful thing! It is our responsibility to help them to know how to properly seek out answers.

Parents must have wisdom to know when our children are ready for certain information. Unfortunately, we live in a culture that is robbing our children of innocence and naivety. There are certain things I wish I didn't have to explain to our children, and there are other things about which I give only the essential information. But the important thing is to be available for all the questions and together navigate how to find the answers.

What prevents curiosity from flourishing?

There are a few barriers to curiosity that we, as adults, should become more aware of as well. Many of these are the same barriers we've talked about in other chapters. Busyness, for example, can prevent many of these gifts from flourishing, even curiosity.

When children are rushing from one activity to another, never allowed to be bored, they simply do not have the time to become curious. Often curiosity is a slow unfolding of a new idea, and that takes time and can easily become squelched with distractions. The constant bombardment of technological stimulation is one such barrier. When my kids are sitting in front of a screen, they aren't asking questions, unless it's to ask for more screen time. They are passively taking in whatever is in front of their eyes.

We are all aware of the dangers of technology. According to Dr. Kathy, "Parents and teens are both affected by the influence of our screen-saturated lives, but young people experience the effects with ferocious intensity."[4] Screens are robbing us of times of mental stillness. But being bored is a good thing, and children today (including mine) struggle if they are not constantly entertained. They have instant access to all kinds of stimulation to the detriment of curiosity.

Technology is not a bad thing. In our family, we use Google and Alexa to answer many, many questions that we have been curious about. We watch documentaries and refer to virtual maps to answer burning questions. But anything good can become a bad thing if overdone or not used within boundaries. And I am the first to admit that we overuse technology at times. It is so convenient in the short term, right? When I am busy and trying to get something done, like writing this book for example, giving my children a device is an easy solution. It keeps them occupied so I can get things done.

But it is not a good long-term solution. Because like you, I want my kids to stay curious. I want them to be bored, and that will involve me being inconvenienced by their sometimes-frustrating behaviors stemming from that boredom. Like today, as I was working on editing this chapter, I encouraged the children to play without screens. I was pleasantly surprised when I didn't hear a lot of bickering or whining. I was not as pleased when I finished my edits and exited my bedroom to see that my living room had been turned into a gigantic fort. It looked like they'd used every sheet in our house to build that thing, experimenting with the perfect configuration as they decided how to create the optimal fort coverage of the living room. The cleanup was not without bickering and whining, but I was glad to see they found ways to stay busy that didn't include a screen. I've found this to be true: when I allow them to be bored long enough, they will find something to be curious about, although it might lead to bigger messes.

Which leads me to another barrier to curiosity: an unwillingness for grown-ups to get a little messy. This can include actual messes, like paint splatters or nature collections filling the kitchen table. Again, everything within boundaries, right? It's a good idea to have a family policy when it comes to curiosity and experimentation. In our home, they know that before they do any major experimenting, like with fire, water, or chemicals, they have to get permission and have an adult supervising. I talk about this more in the chapter on creativity, but clearly communicate boundaries so your children know where and how they are free to explore their creativity without breaking the rules.

Messiness is not only sticky countertops and glitter on the floor; it encompasses messy conversations with sticky subjects and complicated answers.

Sometimes we do not want to make space for questions that don't have neat and tidy answers; we do not want to attempt to address some uncomfortable topics. I understand the fear that may come with hard and messy questions. One example is, of course, talking about sex with our kids. Most parents do not look forward to these awkward conversations. But our children are genuinely curious and need quality information, and they are looking to us for answers. If your child asks a question that you are uncomfortable with, be honest with them—they probably know you're uncomfortable anyway. Find quality sources that can help you walk through those discussions with a little more confidence.

Our culture now is a perfect example of what happens when a generation doesn't know how to navigate difficult conversations and questions, both with respect and critical thinking skills. Adults, especially, argue about topics without first investigating all sides of an issue. They take sound bites (or worse, internet memes) and assume they are factual, further supporting their preconceived notions of what is true. Of course, teaching children how to fact-check takes time. Look at sources with your children; when reading something on the internet, show them how to differentiate quality information from "fake news." Compare headlines on a national news story and note the various ways news outlets cover the same event. Help them to learn to identify fact versus opinion (sometimes it's hard to spot). Discuss how God's Word answers their questions and compare what the Bible says to the world's response. These are all ways we can teach our children how to get quality answers to questions. It takes time and intentionality but is such an important skill to learn and cultivate.

How do we encourage curiosity?

Curiosity is a vital component to critical thinking. It's the ability to analyze and evaluate an issue in order to form an opinion. I would love to see a generation rise up with the ability to analyze and evaluate issues instead of taking sound bites and memes as facts. This begins with learning how to question and evaluate everything, perhaps even questioning things that make us uncomfortable. Some parents may not like the idea of having a teen who questions everything. Much like the toddler who asks "why" a hundred times a day, a teen's questioning may be inconvenient and frustrating, but curiosity is essential to learning and growing!

One of my children tends to question and evaluate (or as I like to call it, challenge) various choices, like why we have to do laundry or dishes instead of playing outside all day. My gut reaction is to say, "Because I said so." Basically, just do what I ask you to do, and it will go well with you, i.e., you will avoid a consequence. But if I want them to continue to question, then I must cultivate their curiosity, and that means taking the time to explain or guiding them in finding the answers for themselves.

If, for example, I say to my daughter, "Why do you think we need to do the dishes and laundry before we can go to the pool with our friends?" she might respond by saying, "Because that's what you said we have to do." When I intentionally foster the quality of curiosity, I help her develop important critical thinking skills that will benefit her in the long run. I can dig deeper and ask, "Why do you think Mommy says that we must do these things?" And eventually, with some prompting, she may get to the fact that we need clean clothes and towels to go to the pool and clean dishes so we can pack our picnic. Eventually, she will begin to understand the logic behind rules.

This practice takes patience and time and possibly a shift in our priorities.

Encouraging curiosity, as well as the other eleven qualities, means that we must have a clear understanding of what parental authority looks like. Our parental authority comes from God. This does not give us permission to be heartless dictators. We must establish a healthy and biblical understanding of submission to the authorities God places over us while also teaching our children how to discern when to question injustice and when to stand for what is right. By modeling appropriate authority, we teach our children how to recognize positive and negative types of leadership.

If my primary objective is to raise obedient children who just do what I say, then telling them "because I said so" would work out just fine in the short term. But if I take a longer view of parenting, and my priority is to raise adults who think critically by evaluating, analyzing, and questioning the world around them, then I will be willing to take the time to encourage this God-given quality in them now, no matter how frustrating and time-consuming and inconvenient it may be.

There is an old belief that we should not question authority, Scripture, and definitely not God. However, God encourages us to humbly and honestly approach Him with our questions, and He is always ready to provide answers. He is the perfect Father who encourages curiosity in His children and desires for them to come to Him for answers. It is through these questions that we, His children, get to know Him and His creation even better. May it never be said that we have arrived at all knowledge and understanding, but may we continue to be humble and acknowledge how little we truly know. May we be hungry to know more, and may our children see that and follow in our footsteps.

It is not just enough to encourage them to question everything. They must see us do this too.

Remember, "more is caught than taught," and just like any of these qualities, curiosity must be modeled if we want our children to value it. Parents must become lifelong learners who remain curious. We must be willing to investigate things that might make us uncomfortable in order to gain a better understanding.

Recently, I read a book that challenged my view of the death penalty and racial bias in the criminal justice system.[5] Anytime our beliefs are challenged, we can feel uncomfortably stretched because we are confident in our beliefs and uneasy when those beliefs are contested. I'm still not sure exactly what I think on this topic of the death penalty, but I want my children to see that I am always learning and challenging my understanding on issues. We don't want to model a close-minded perspective that makes us unable to discuss various sides of an issue. Instead, the goal is to teach them to evaluate all sides of an issue in order to come to a more complete understanding.

Again, this takes focus and time; it can be difficult. But it's good not only for our children to see us modeling curiosity but good for us too!

We were created with a brain that thrives on learning new things. Research suggests that adults who continue to learn and strengthen their brain are able to continue to use their brains much longer than those who stop learning and stretching their minds.[6] And isn't it just like God, to allow us as parents to do something that is both good for us and good for our kids?

Even the smartest people in the world would admit that there is much they don't know. These are the people who remain curious, who are constantly seeking to learn and grow in knowledge and who are willing to change their opinion when they are given new information. We talked about flexible thinking and not being stuck in fixed ways of thinking; curiosity and flexibility go hand in hand.

And not only flexibility, but inventiveness and curiosity work in tandem as well! It is this quality of curiosity that leads to innovation and discovery . . . something our world desperately needs. One surprising statistic shows that 65 percent of children in school today will be working in jobs that do not even exist yet.[7]

What should not be surprising given the advances in technology just over the past forty years is that innovation will continue to explode. And our children are going to be a part of that innovative work force. What better way to prepare them for the future than to foster this quality of curiosity so that perhaps they will be on the forefront of that innovation.

But if they are not encouraged to question and evaluate and analyze, if they do not become lifelong learners, then I am afraid they will not be able to fulfill their God-given potential. I know that each of our children are created with a unique purpose and calling. Our job as parents is to cultivate all their unique skills and qualities to prepare them for the future God has in store. Allowing them to maintain a love of learning and curiosity is vital to their reaching their highest potential.

To summarize, here are some practical ways to do just that:

1. Encourage and allow your children to ask questions and be curious. Provide a safe and loving place for them to come with all their questions.
2. Be a role model of curiosity. Continue to learn new things and share that love with your children.
3. Provide plenty of opportunity for experiences that will spark curiosity.
4. Study your child and find out what they are curious about and be curious along with them.

The good news is that you are probably already doing some of this but not realizing how much you are sparking curiosity.

Chapter 8

Creativity

It was a few days before Easter in 2020. We had been stuck inside for quite some time, and we were running out of ways to keep the kids busy. Maybe I'd seen something online—I'm not sure where the idea came from. And thanks to Dr. Kathy and my newfound fascination with these qualities, I was ready to say yes to more experiences that sparked these qualities.

Well, you should have seen John's face as he walked into the dining room that day. Our huge window overlooking the front yard was covered in paint. Tape marked off areas where the paint would go. From the front of the house, he could see our artwork in progress; but when he entered the dining room, he could see the mess that was made in the creating process.

In years past, if John had walked into a mess like that, with paint on a window and duct tape everywhere, he would have been annoyed and probably a little irritated with me. But because of Dr. Kathy's influence on our family and our growing appreciation for these God-given qualities that we were encouraging in our home, John wasn't even fazed at all. In fact, he was proud of our work. He took pictures and even shared them with Kathy. I am thankful that as a family we were able to embrace this gift of creativity, and we enjoyed that artwork way past Easter!

WHAT IS CREATIVITY?

Creativity is "the ability to make or otherwise bring into existence something new."[1] Armstrong views creativity as "the capacity to give birth to new ways of looking at things."[2] Creativity encompasses original thought, as Armstrong suggests, but I believe it is much more. Creativity is an ability and desire to make something that is uniquely our own. Bringing something new into existence or giving birth to something new, a creative idea or an artistic endeavor, points to the ultimate life-giver, Creator God. Genesis 1 tells us that He brought the world into existence from nothing, creating everything, including humanity. His creativity that He imparted to us sets humanity apart from the rest of creation. Only we are made in His image!

Creativity not only makes us distinctly human; it is also good for us. Creativity promotes overall well-being.[3] When we create, whether it's painting, coloring, or composing music, our bodies experience feel-good chemicals. This is why creative outlets are usually encouraged for people experiencing depression or anxiety. It is therapeutic. The reverse is also true: the more stressed we are, the less creativity flows.

Creativity is not only good for our mental health, but it is good for business too! According to Harvard Business School, creativity "not only combats stagnation but facilitates growth and innovation."[4] Employers are looking for creative employees who can bring new ideas and solutions to the workplace. And this creativity is imparted in each of us. Our children are bubbling with it, but where does all that creativity go?

What happens to creativity over time?

Much has been written about our decline in creativity. One key study evaluated creativity in 1,600 children at various ages. George Land and Beth Jarman noted that at the age of five years old, "98 percent of children in the study scored as highly creative," at a genius level of creativity.[5] When the children were reevaluated five years later, the study showed the number had dropped to 30 percent; and even lower by age fifteen to only 12 percent. By the time these children reached adulthood, only 2 percent scored high on the creativity index.

We have probably noticed this decline in ourselves and in our own children. So why the drastic change? The researchers in this longitudinal study suggest that it is childlike playfulness that allows creativity to thrive. As children mature, they lose the free time and uninhibitedness that comes with childhood playfulness. They stop playing. They begin to worry about if their drawings are "good enough," instead of just creating for the fun of it.

How do we encourage creativity in our homes?

Can you picture one of your children when they first discovered coloring? Once they have learned the joy of coloring, they can't stop the desire to create, sometimes to the detriment of our walls. Every one of our four children attempted to color on the walls. This was not something we taught them (or allowed). As soon as they learned how to hold a crayon (or Sharpie in one instance), a blank wall became an enticing canvas on which to express themselves. Has this ever happened in your home?

Children love to create all kinds of things. The child who discovers coloring had to first learn a few skills. They needed to be able to hold the crayon, and they had to understand how to press the crayon down hard enough to leave a mark. No artistic master, whether a sculptor, painter, or composer, creates masterpieces without first having been exposed to the basics in their field. To create something, people first need exposure to ideas and experience using different tools. I recently taught my daughters how to crotchet. Before they learned the basics of choosing the right size needle and yarn and a few easy stitches, they could not create a single recognizable item. Because they were exposed to these basics and I patiently walked them through each step, they can now make some pretty cute things.

We simply expose our children to a variety of experiences and information, and creativity blossoms. Watch stage plays with your children, visit different kinds of art museums, listen to classical music. Each child is designed uniquely, with different passions and purposes. In helping a child try a variety of new things, we are also guiding them into discovering their own gifts and purposes, the special way they are meant to create.

Experience is not the only prerequisite for creativity. Space and freedom for creative expression are also vital. A child who is constantly distracted, bombarded with stimulation, never has an opportunity to be still or bored, and isn't given space to allow creativity to flourish will not cultivate creativity. Are you a family constantly on the go, or do you have plenty of free time? Free time is a necessity we rarely allow ourselves; however, it is essential to the nurture of so many of the qualities, especially curiosity.

But it's not just downtime or boredom that is necessary; a child needs to feel safe in knowing they have the freedom to create. Children need to understand, within boundaries, where and with what they are free to express their creativity.

In our home, we keep a box of papers, cardboard pieces, felt, crayons, pencils, a hot glue gun, and many other random items. My daughters know that anything that is put inside that box is free for them to use for creative expression. I took time to explain a few times what our house rules were regarding creativity, and those rules look different in each home. For us, if they aren't damaging walls, furniture, or each other, our children are allowed to make a mess. They also have to clean it up (which to be honest is the biggest struggle for them!). They create all sorts of things: treasure maps and scavenger hunts, outfits for dolls, and accessories for their bedrooms, whatever their creative minds can come up with. They know that I won't get mad if they cut up socks; if the socks are in "the box," they know these items are theirs to do with what they want. Sometimes, when they find things they would like to put in the box, I usually say yes.

Children who have parents who value creativity are much more likely to be creative themselves. And creativity doesn't have to only be an arts and crafts type of creating. Does your family value creativity? Do you share with your child any of your creative passions? What type of creativity do you notice in your child? Creativity in writing and storytelling, in making up songs, in arranging furniture and decorating their bedroom? Do they solve problems creatively or are they always inventing solutions to problems? Creativity is found everywhere.

Our family loves creating music. We have guitars, keyboards, and an Alexa that blasts a variety of music. Both John and I love music; he was a vocal music major in college, so music is a part of our family culture. We watch musicals together and sing along at the top of our lungs. Not every child is musically gifted, but as a family we all appreciate making a joyful noise. What is your family's creative passion? Do you make time for it as a family?

Ultimately, we decided that we are willing to be inconvenienced, allowing messes and noisy instruments, knowing that their creative expression is worth so much more than a clean dining room table or a quiet house! Remember, short-term sacrifice for long-term gain should be our goal. If I choose to get frustrated with scraps of paper all over the floor (oh, the endless messes), if I am not willing to listen to a new song they wrote (because let's be honest, it is not always enjoyable), I discourage creativity. Even if I do not outwardly express my frustration, they know when I am irritated by their messes and noises; kids are good at reading us (part of the quality of sensitivity). If instead I choose to celebrate what they do, to participate in the creating by coming alongside them—not taking over a project but simply enjoying watching the creative process—it will do wonders for their confidence and their overall enjoyment. I know it's not always easy, and it's definitely not convenient, but I hope that you are starting to see the value of choosing to parent this way.

Will you decide to allow for creativity even if it means a painted window and some duct tape? Will you choose to see the beautiful creation as a masterpiece instead of just a mess? I know I am glad that we have chosen this perspective. And I believe you will be glad if you do too!

Chapter 9

Imagination

Close your eyes and picture your favorite place in the world. Imagine the sights and sounds and maybe even the smells. Is it a beach with sunshine and sand, sounds of crashing waves in front of you, and seagulls squawking overhead? Or maybe it's a quiet mountain scene, with a bubbling brook and the scent of pine and earth. Can you picture who you would want with you there? A face you can make out in your mind. Their smile, the way the light hits their features, and the way their presence makes you feel. If you were able to picture this, then you have the God-given quality of imagination. The truth is every human ever born has this gift! It is such a wonderful part of being human. It is one of the very things that sets us apart from any other species—our ability to use imagination, to picture things in our mind.

WHAT IS IMAGINATION?

Imagination is a hallmark of childhood. As your child plays dress up, pretends to care for baby dolls, or takes on the role of a police officer who arrests bad guys, they are trying on roles, practicing how to express emotions, and imagining their future.[1] Imagination allows us to put ourselves in stories or places we never may have been. Armstrong defines imagination as the child's ability "to close their eyes and see all sorts of images."[2] With our imagination we can "see" stories unfold in our minds.

Thanks to rich descriptions in God's Word, pictures are painted that allow us to imagine. This makes me think of one of my favorite Christian songs by the band MercyMe, "I Can Only Imagine," and thanks to imagination, with God's Word, we *can* imagine. Imagination enhances worship; we imagine as we pray; we picture the stories of the Bible as they play out on the screens of our mind. Jesus was a master of painting pictures, evoking the imagination of His listeners as He told parables. Jesus describes what the kingdom of heaven is like in Matthew 13, and we can picture the merchant finding the pearl of great price. In our minds, we see him excitedly selling everything he has to buy this precious shiny pearl. Jesus created us with an imagination and uses that to help us see His stories unfold and see our place in those stories. This quality of imagination draws us closer to God Himself, as He intended.

Imagination not only helps us connect with God, it allows us to empathize with others. We can put ourselves in others' shoes, even those who are different from us. By doing that, we can start to understand the world from another person's perspective. Children who practice the important skill of imagining a different point of view grow up to be more empathic.[3]

When asked if he trusted imagination over knowledge, Albert Einstein said that "imagination is more important than knowledge. Knowledge is limited. Imagination encircles the world."[4] Einstein relied on his imagination when discovering scientific breakthroughs. He wrote that "to raise new questions, new possibilities, to regard old problems from a new angle, requires creative imagination and marks real advance in science."[5] And he wasn't the only scientist that dreamed up ideas that led to major scientific discoveries.[6] Imagination is essential to discovering the unknown. Our children must first be able to imagine what *could* be in order to create something new.

Imagination not only helps further scientific breakthroughs, it also provides an outlet for dreams. Daydreaming, while sometimes considered a waste of time, is actually beneficial. "Mind wandering" can increase creativity and problem-solving in students.[7] When allowed to dream about their future, our children will be able to more clearly articulate their goals. In dreaming, they can allow the Holy Spirit to open their eyes to a calling they hadn't yet imagined! That is what I want for my children, dreams inspired by the Holy Spirit, and I bet you do too.

What makes it difficult for imagination to flourish?

If we agree that imagination is essential, why does it seem to become less important? As we age, childlike imagination becomes less of a priority. We no longer dream about fairy-tale lands, unless encouraged and allowed to. This beautiful gift of imagination is used less and less over time. Neuroscientists demonstrate that like a muscle we don't use regularly, vivid visual imaginations get weaker and less frequent over time.[8]

By the time our children become preteens and teenagers, imagination takes a back seat in most schools. Armstrong strongly argued that "the main reason the imagination is absent from nearly all classrooms today is that there is no room for it anywhere in the curriculum."[9] Even though scientific geniuses like Einstein view imagination as essential in education, the typical school curriculum today minimizes it, prioritizing instead memorizing facts. There is little time built in for free, imaginative play. As early as kindergarten in some school districts, imaginative activities are replaced with sight word memorization and handwriting centers. Emphasis is placed on passing standardized tests instead of celebrating imagination, innovation, and creativity. Even creative writing classes don't always allow for true, unbridled imagination because homework assignments can impose boundaries that help ensure school district checklists are covered. I bet if you thought back to your favorite teachers in school, they were likely the ones who sparked your imagination in some way. My favorite teachers read great fiction out loud, and one used voices to act out the many characters in the story. We may not have control over how our schools educate (unless you choose to homeschool), but we can encourage imagination outside of classroom time.

In the average American home, things do not get much better when children get home from school. They are bombarded with screens, extracurricular activities, homework, and no time to simply daydream. We are seeing distractions steal imagination from children younger and younger. If our children do not have the time and space to imagine . . . they won't.

We have the power to control our children's schedule while they are in our homes. We can decide what activities are important and what we can lay aside for a season in order to allow more free time. We set the limits on technology use. While handing our children a screen to entertain them may keep them busy and preoccupied, this will not cultivate imagination quite like a good story or daydreaming will.

Sitting down as a family to read a book takes time and patience. Inevitably someone will be unhappy with the story that was chosen, and someone else will need to go to the bathroom, causing everyone else to grumble about Mom pausing the story (I know from experience). You might consider giving up on the whole reading out loud thing altogether and just give in to the devices that are tempting ways to keep the kids quiet. However, remembering why we chose to parent inconveniently— why we know sparking imagination is worthwhile—will help us persevere on those hard days. And maybe you can even use different voices, like my favorite teacher did, to really cultivate imagination!

How do we encourage imagination in our children?

We all want for our children to have rich imaginations that will help them see into the unknown future and envision all that God has in store. We must make time for imagination. When kids are younger, this looks like having unstructured play time. Children need access to many types of objects and the freedom to do with them what they will. Their imaginations can soar with a simple stick, but the more quality toys we can offer the more they will engage in imaginative play. Obviously, keeping children safe is a priority; being rough or dangerous in free play is never acceptable. For the most part, children will not need any directions or modeling for imaginative play; they will just do what comes naturally and let their imaginations go wild.

If your children are a little older and have not had a lot of opportunity for imaginative play, then it could be you haven't been modeling this for them. Watching Mom or Dad pretend to be a pirate or a cowboy, maybe on an alien planet, using a banana as a way to communicate, will inspire children to join and add to the fun. It is always a great way to strengthen relationships and make wonderful family memories!

We will talk more later about the importance of fun and how vital playfulness is in our children and in our homes, but for now, just understand that imagination blooms best in the soil of fun and play. When children feel safe and are allowed to be silly, their imaginations soar. Some homes are rigid with rules; and while rules are healthy and necessary, when overused they can stifle many essential qualities our children need in order to grow into the adults God intends them to be. We need to evaluate which rules are necessary and appropriate, or which we may be using for our own convenience.

Employing a blanket rule is easier than being present and teaching our children how to wisely discern when it's acceptable to do different things. For example, for a long time a rule in our house was "no playing ball inside, ever." It was a rule my parents had for me as a child, and it made sense—throwing balls leads to breaking things and that is not acceptable. But when we began homeschooling and spending a lot more time indoors, I realized that "no playing ball inside, ever" wasn't very practical. We used balls for science experiments and to entertain toddlers and puppies.

My kids have learned that they can be active in the house, throw balls, and even shoot suction cup arrows at the sliding glass door if they are also acting sensibly and responsibly. They also know that accidents happen, and I choose to give grace if things accidentally get broken. We work together to figure out a way to fix whatever has been broken. Sometimes that means super glue, and sometimes that means using birthday money to replace it. This approach can help our children learn how to discern wisely for themselves and gives them the comfort in knowing they have the freedom to be children, to be human, and to make mistakes. The alternative is children who are trying to function in a home of fear and perfection.

A motto in our house is "people over things," and I have to remind myself of that sometimes, especially when things get broken. I must choose grace and forgiveness if I want to create a home that allows my children to flourish. Because the truth is, I will need that same grace and forgiveness myself.

Now, there are some children who are created with an extra dose of imagination, and no matter what is going on, they will be imagining things all day long. These children are such a treasure, and while it might be tempting to use the old adage "get your head out of the clouds," I pray that we do not. Instead, we can choose to see their imaginations as a blessing from God. Do you have a very imaginative child? Celebrate them.

One of my daughters loves to play dolls. She pretends she is mom to eight babies; all adopted, she will tell you. She is always asking her father and me to help care for the granddaughters. As I'm writing this, I have a baby doll propped up next to me that I am "babysitting." My daughter especially loves to bring her dolls with her whenever we leave the house. I limit her to only two babies per outing; eight would be too much to manage. She brings her double stroller, diaper bag packed with extra clothes and diapers, and the baby car seat. It takes extra time to get in and out of the car with this young mom and her two babies, but I do it because I want her to make believe. I know that the day will come when she no longer wants to pretend with baby dolls. Until then I will "babysit" and pretend to be Grandma, I will be okay with walking a little slower around the neighborhood because she's pushing the baby stroller, and I will encourage her to keep pretending.

There are so many ways to spark imagination in your children. Besides joining in with your children in imaginative play, you can play games as a family that ignite imagination. One game we like to play doesn't even have a name, but we just pretend that an object around the house is something else. We take turns imagining what the "thing" could be, and we keep going until we run out of ideas. A shoe could be a phone or a sea creature or a hat or a dog toy or a portal to another dimension. We let our imaginations run wild, and we never criticize someone for their ideas. Nothing is off limits, as long as it's appropriate. I add the "as long as it's appropriate" caveat because after studying human anatomy in school, our youngest daughter was fixated on certain body parts, and we had to consistently remind her it wasn't appropriate to discuss apart from science class. We didn't want to shame her, but instead wanted to help her understand that certain topics are not for play but for educational conversations only. I did not want her going to church on Wednesday night and playing with her friends and bringing up anatomy parts thinking she was being imaginative!

We as parents should celebrate all forms of imagination and demonstrate its importance by making it part of our lives too. This does not have to look the same for everyone, but we all have the ability to imagine. And above all else, we can use our imagination as we read Scripture and as we worship God with our hearts, souls, bodies, and minds. It is this worship through the mind that utilizes the gift of imagination. Not only is it a good idea but it's also commanded in Scripture. In Matthew 22:37, Jesus told us that the greatest commandment is to love the Lord our God with all our heart, soul, and mind—this involves our imagination. So, the next time you are reading Scripture and you can picture the story as if you are there, or you are able to draw a picture in your mind of heaven or creation as you read the Psalms, thank God for imagination and ask Him to help you encourage it in your home.

Chapter 10

Inventiveness

My daughters are always coming up with new and inventive ways to use everyday objects. My measuring cups, for example, can be found everywhere except the kitchen drawer in which they belong. This can prove very inconvenient when I am trying to measure an ingredient for a recipe and the two-thirds cup measurer is missing!

Instead, these cups are used to scoop things up or to carry water somewhere. They have been used as building blocks for a cup tower, a bathtub for a doll, and containers for craft beads. While these ideas may not seem as innovative as the printing press, they are small ways that my girls have created something new to help them solve a problem they encounter.

Measuring cups aren't the only things they repurpose. Old boxes are constantly turned into something new—dog houses and rocket ships, hamster mazes and castles. Their imagination leads to all kinds of inventive creations. Is my house a mess at times with "castles" cluttering up the living room? Definitely! Do I have to remind them often to clean up their inventions after they are finished creating? For sure. But when I consider the long-term goal of raising innovative thinkers, it makes up for the mess and inconvenience.

WHAT IS INVENTIVENESS?

Inventiveness is the combination of curiosity, creativity, and imagination to make something entirely new—like my girls do with measuring cups and old boxes. *Merriam-Webster* defines it as productive imagination.[1]

Inventions have changed the course of history: the light bulb, the printing press, the airplane, computers . . . all these inventions began in the curious mind of an inventor, someone who recognized a need, dreamed up an idea, and worked to produce it. Who comes to mind when I mention inventors? Johannes Gutenberg creating his incredible printing press, or George Washington Carver dreaming up many new uses for the peanut. Invention begins long before a final product is created. The exciting thing is that oftentimes inventions begin with curiosity or a determination to create something new to solve a problem—and questions and problems are all around us. We can help our children take notice of those questions and problems and then give them space and freedom to come up with creative solutions.

It doesn't have to be a world-changing invention for us to see inventiveness at work. We can see it in our children daily if we know what to look for. Do your children come up with silly ways to say words? Do they make new things out of their plate of peas? Maybe you see it in the unusual way they want to play a game, not by the rules but by rules of their own making. This happens at our house and can lead to lots of fighting. Rigid-thinking, sometimes inflexible children don't typically like to come up with creative rules to games. But it is such good practice for flexibility, which leads to creativity and inventiveness, that enduring a grumpy attitude can be worth it because eventually a child may find fun in the new and different mindset. This is just one way we can encourage inventiveness.

The future is ripe with inventions not dreamed up yet. Our children will be that future and the future is changing at a rapid pace. If we want to help our children to be leaders of the future, then inventiveness is one of the keys to their success!

What prevents us from encouraging this gift?

For starters, inventiveness cannot occur without curiosity, creativity, and imagination being ignited as well. Much like the other qualities, a child must have the time and space to wonder about a problem and have the confidence in themselves to create a solution to a problem. But without first noticing a problem, would there a be need for a solution? Too often as parents, we try to solve problems for our children before they have a chance to struggle for a solution themselves; we want to fix things before they even realize there is a problem.

I know I am guilty of this. Especially when my firstborn, Joey, was a toddler. I was so afraid of anything happening to him that I rarely let him experience things for himself. I anxiously followed around the playground. I was the epitome of a helicopter mom, hovering over him to ensure he was safe at all times. One day, I was at the park chatting with a friend, and I noticed that Joey wouldn't go play with the other children. He was so afraid of getting hurt that he just stood by me. As much as I tried to encourage him to play, assuring him he would be okay, he would not budge. In that moment, I realized my desire to protect him communicated that I didn't trust that he could manage on his own, that my desire to keep him safe was most important. That day I decided to stop jumping in every time I thought he was in danger. Of course, I was close enough to protect him if he truly was unsafe, but I gave him room to find his own way and that made all the difference. By the time my youngest was toddling around the playground, she was full of confidence and scaling walls that I would've never let Joey attempt. And she's found her strength and confidence to overcome obstacles because I gave her the room to find her footing and test her strength.

Thanks to the lessons I learned early on, as Joey has become older, he too has learned to be confident in his ability to problem-solve. We have let him fail and fall down so that he learns he is capable of getting back up. It is not always easy watching our children struggle. We want to jump in and rescue them. But it is in the struggle that they learn resilience and the ability to come up with solutions.

One day I was driving to church—alone, which is rare for me— and listening to Dr. Kathy's *Celebrate Kids* podcast. I heard the most incredible story.[2] Did you know that scientists in Arizona created a biosphere—an enclosed dome that originally attempted to replicate earth's environment? They wanted to study ecosystems in a closed and scientific manner. What they did not anticipate was the importance of wind resistance on the environment. What they discovered was that the trees needed to build up resistance to the wind in order to grow taller and stronger with deep roots. Without the wind, they were weak and prone to fall over. Why am I telling you about a scientific biosphere? First, because I think it's fascinating how God created our earth to function, each piece playing an essential part, and that includes you and me and our children too. But I also share this because just like those trees, our children need some resistance to build the muscles to endure, to push through obstacles, and to find innovative solutions.

If we want to raise our children to become adults who fulfill their God-given purposes, then we must take God's Word to heart and trust that some trials and difficulties are good for them. The first chapter of James reminds us that we should count it all joy when we (or our children) face various trials because we know that the testing of our faith (or the strengthening of our faith muscles) develops perseverance, and perseverance is necessary for maturity in faith and in life (see James 1:2–4).

By fixing problems for our children rather than allowing them to problem-solve their own solutions, we risk raising a generation of children that don't have this resilience or ability to grow through obstacles. In doing this, parents limit the creative problem-solving skills that need to be cultivated. Allowing our children to work to overcome and problem-solve strengthens their flexible thinking, which allows room for creative solutions to those problems. Dr. Kathy writes, "Successfully walking out of valleys and navigating struggles results in a solution-focused mindset."[3] Those creative solutions are the products of their imagination—that is inventiveness.

What can we do to bring inventiveness back into our homes?

Here is where it can become inconvenient and messy. In order to encourage our children to be inventive, we must be willing to give them freedom to create new things. Much like encouraging creativity, we can't be afraid of a little messiness. Having a box of old items that are safe things to use to invent with is a great way to have boundaries while allowing for freedom. And we have to get over the idea that our homes should be Pinterest-worthy at all times. We need to decide to be okay with extra clutter.

Prioritize slowing down and providing opportunities for inventiveness.

Designate zones for creating and inventing.

Provide plenty of random items and discarded supplies that can be repurposed for new uses, but make sure to communicate boundaries that allow freedom to create and invent. If you have discussions with your children about what is allowed and what is off limits, as well as the best way for your child to ask when inspiration strikes, they will want to invent something. Decide ahead of time how this would work best for your family so that your home is a fertile ground for creativity, imagination, and invention.

Chapter 11

Playfulness

I walked into the brightly lit kitchen where John, with a peculiar smirk, scurried away from the kitchen sink. I knew something was up. As soon as I turned on the faucet, I knew why John had that mischievous grin. He had turned the faucet handle around and had the sprayer button primed and ready so that as soon as I turned the water on, I got a face soaked with water!

In that moment, the whole household seemed to hold their breath. Waiting. Wondering what would happen next. Would I get irritated at the mess and get angry with John for playing a prank on me? All too often, that is my natural reaction to such pranks. But that day was different. I decided to embrace the fun, and I turned the sprayer on everyone else. I started with soaking John. He was the instigator, after all. But I didn't stop there. Any child within range of the sprayer got wet. Giggles erupted.

Joey broke out the super soaker and the water battle got serious! We had a mess to clean up, and I am fairly sure somebody slipped on the tile floor because of the water. But when I think back to that day, all I remember is the fun. And I know the children do too!

WHAT IS PLAYFULNESS?

Playfulness is "an attitude toward life."[1] A playful attitude finds fun around every corner. Just like John's mischief in the kitchen, playfulness can be infused anywhere. The way we smile at others, the way we skip down the street, playfulness shows up. We see playfulness most keenly in young children. It is a natural part of learning and development. Through play, children get to try on different roles and practice new skills.[2] Just like with imagination, play allows children to become different people and "visit" faraway places and eras. Today my youngest daughters sipped tea and played with beautiful, folded fans as they imagined themselves in ancient China, all from the living room. While children naturally are drawn toward it, playfulness is not just for kids.

During play, parts of the brain that overanalyze and overthink are turned down, and creativity is unlocked and set free. It is during times of playfulness that we are most open to learning and trying new things because there are less inhibitions. Children don't worry about "doing it wrong" while being playful; they are just having fun. And of course, play makes for great memories and bonding.

Some of my best childhood memories are centered around playing with Barbie dolls with my sister and cousins, building sandcastles on the beach, and imagining the castles being invaded by pirates. I'm sure you could say the same about your childhood memories. Play is such a memorable part of childhood.

Play also incorporates many of the qualities we have already discussed. In play, creativity soars, flexible thinking is more likely to occur because of the relaxed state, vitality is sparked, and we experience innovative ideas during playful times. Armstrong wrote that "when children play, they take what 'is,' combine it with what is 'possible' in their imagination, and from this transformation create something new."[3] Much research has been done showing that play is the "way children integrate all of their learning,"[4] and according to the American Academy of Pediatrics, play is practicing that is fun.

Play is good for us and good for our children! Much like the spoonful of sugar that helps the medicine go down, playfulness can help bring sweetness to a difficult day. Playfulness provides stress relief and a release of feel-good hormones. Research on college-age students found the higher level of playfulness, the lower level of perceived stress.[5] This attitude of fun toward life helps us cope with stress.

God, in His wisdom, knew at creation that play was beneficial physically and emotionally . . . and it is just plain fun. All creatures have a tendency toward play. As children, play is our first, and best, form of learning. It is in play that we are relaxed, and our thinking is most fluid and easily expressed. There are many benefits to play. Playfulness protects against stress, helps build bonds, and teaches us not to take life too seriously. In play, children don't feel the pressure to perform, so they are more likely to try new or hard things, which helps build resiliency and flexibility. Scripture tells us what science has studied for decades, "a joyful heart is good medicine."[6]

When did play become something we have to earn or make time for? When did playfulness take a back seat in childhood instead of being a vital part of daily life for children?

Unfortunately, culture tells us other things are more important: academics, success in sports, responsibilities, and activities. Much like with imagination, schools no longer prioritize playfulness and instead focus on passing standardized tests. We need to balance our schedules to make sure our children—and we, too—have margin for play.

Sometimes our children don't play because they are so stressed out and drained from the busyness of life and expectations placed upon them that they don't have time or even the desire to be playful. If we are not careful, our children can become depressed, anxious, and overwhelmed. They may lose the desire to play and eventually their spark for life! The statistics are staggering when it comes to mental health issues among children today. The rates for depression and anxiety among children ages six to seventeen increased steadily from only 5 percent in 2003 to over 8 percent in 2012, and over 12 percent from 2016–2019.[7] And things haven't gotten better since 2019.

Obviously, there are many factors that contribute to these sad statistics, but the reality is that parents can be on the front lines helping curb this rising trend. God has placed the family as the haven where children's needs can be met. We can decide, with prayer and discernment, what our family's priorities should be instead of what culture tells us should matter. And I hope that playfulness is a family priority! As we will discuss later, many things can be approached playfully if we have the right attitude. This is how we can usher in playfulness to our homes.

Besides choosing to prioritize play we must change our perception of the playful child. One perception is that playful kids are misbehaving. These playful kids want everything to be a game or a competition. Especially in classroom settings, but even at home, it can be frustrating trying to get these children to focus and be serious. Have you experienced this with any of your children? My daughters always want everything to be a game. Especially when we have "table time" where the kids must complete assignments, I am not in the mood to play. But what if these playful children just need *more* time to play, to be kids? After a particularly hard day of homeschooling, I sat my children down and asked them why they were complaining and not being cooperative. One daughter bluntly stated that school was boring; she hated sitting still. My gut reaction was to tell her in my mean mom voice that sometimes we have to do boring things like sitting still when we don't want to. Instead, I took a few breaths and calmly asked her how she would do school if she were in charge. I reminded her that we have to get assignments done, but what would she do differently? She came up with a brilliant idea. She said we could set a timer for thirty minutes, and when the timer went off, we could run around the backyard or dance to a fun song for ten minutes. Once we got the wiggles out, we could come back to the table work and start the timer all over again. We implemented this idea of fun, and it worked great. We started having less grumbling and more cooperation.

That is probably true for most kids. A lot of the behavior issues we see in schools and at home could be alleviated if children had more time to be playful. We must embrace the playful attitudes toward life, not as a problem to deal with but as a gift to treasure.

How can we be intentional about bringing more play into our homes?

Once we decide that playfulness is an important part of childhood and that we want to prioritize it in our homes, the fun part can begin! Any situation can become playful if we decide to have a playful attitude. Turning a household chore into a dance party is a sure way to usher in fun. Know your family. Know your child. Smile more. Do a challenging crossword puzzle and use colored pens for each word to make it playful. For some, telling silly jokes may be their idea of fun. You are the expert on your family, so figure out what is playful and choose to do more of that!

Invite the Lord to help you develop this attitude in yourself and in your home. Remember playfulness was His good idea. A playful person expresses a hope and joy unbridled by stress and worry. When we can truly relax, knowing that God is in control, we have the freedom to enjoy life! Isn't that what we want for our children? No matter what difficulties may come, we want them to have hope for tomorrow that allows them to experience a light heart today. This starts with us. We need to have this hope so that, like the woman described in Proverbs 31, we can smile at the future.[8] And smiles are contagious.

There is no right or wrong way to be playful. If you make space for playfulness, if you encourage it by joining in on the fun (like I chose to that day in the kitchen), you will be amazed at how playfulness can be sparked in your family!

Chapter 12

Humor

It was one of those heavy, somber days. Dear friends of ours were in court for their foster daughter's hearing. They asked me to join them. I wasn't entirely sure what to expect, but I was honored to offer moral support and prayer alongside them. We had already walked some of the difficult road of foster care with them, and this day was *the* day that they were asked to testify on behalf of their foster daughter in the trial for the termination of the rights of her biological parents. It was a heart-breaking day because a woman was coming into court as a mother and would most likely be leaving court no longer considered a parent. While our friends wanted the best for their foster daughter, their hearts were breaking for the biological mother as they watched a family legally be terminated. At this point, you are probably wondering why in the world I would start a chapter on the gift of humor with such a heavy story.

It was on this stressful day that I experienced firsthand the gift that is humor. I will never forget walking up and down the hallway of the court-house that morning, side by side with my friend, not sure what to say or how to pray for her and anxious about what was to come. Knowing my friend was nervous about testifying and struggling with the desire to protect this baby girl they had come to love while also grieving for this mother who was losing her rights, I could feel the tension in the hallway! I can still remember the narrow hallway with the worn carpet and the faded wallpaper. I remember the large, framed pictures on the walls. As we paced and prayed, one of the black-and-white pictures caught our attention. I don't even remember what it was about that particular picture that we'd noticed. But for some reason we thought it was so funny! I remember laughing so hard that we both had tears running down our cheeks. I remember thinking, we should not be laughing right now, but it also felt good to lighten the mood. I was thankful for that laughter and a little levity in a serious situation; I was also thankful we didn't get in trouble for giggling so loudly in the courthouse. I half-expected a bailiff to come and tell us to be quiet, which probably would've made us laugh all the more.

WHAT IS HUMOR?

Mark Twain wrote: "Humor is the greatest thing, the saving thing, after all. The minute it crops up, all our hardnesses yield, all our irritations and resentments flit away, and a sunny spirit takes their place."[1] Humor is God's gift to us. It is a way to release tension and bring joy.

Humor is defined as the capacity to express or perceive what is funny. This capacity begins to develop at an early age. Infants form a sense of humor by watching how others respond to their different behaviors.

We are hardwired with the ability to notice funny things and to respond with laughter. As far back as ancient Greece, we can find examples of comedy. Aristotle was a proponent of the benefits of humor, and a brief survey of the history of comedy reveals that humor is a fundamental part of human nature. Although we may not agree on whether something is funny, we can all point to something we perceive as humorous.

As I studied humor, I was not surprised to discover that humor, much like playfulness, benefits our families in many ways. Did you know that a sense of humor is your mind's immune system protecting against unhealthy ways of coping? Humor acts as a sort of emotional filter that helps refine negative experiences into a more humorous light. Humor helps us not take ourselves too seriously, and therefore helps prevent unhealthy side effects of stress, like burnout or anxiety or depression. Humor has been shown to improve the quality of life for those suffering with chronic illnesses and, for some, even improves the conditions. Scientists have discovered the many health benefits of humor, including improved cardiovascular health, decreased stress levels, and increased serotonin levels in the brain.[2]

My wise friend Sally Baucke explained that she uses humor as a nurse. She tells funny jokes while prepping patients for difficult procedures in order to brighten their days and lessen their suffering. Did you know there is science behind the good feelings all that laughter provides? Research supports the idea that laughter produces endorphins, which makes difficult, even painful, medical procedures seem less painful and more tolerable to patients.[3] Researchers have discovered what God knew from the beginning of creation: laughter and a cheerful heart are good medicine.[4]

But humor is not only good for reducing stress and improving heart health; it is also good for improving focus and decision-making. Humor inspires creativity and connectedness. Humor also has been shown to improve workplace environments. Researchers have found that the best bosses have a management style the uses positive forms of humor.[5]

There are many types of humor, and not all humor is beneficial. Some humor is even hurtful. If you've ever been the brunt of someone's joke, you know what I am talking about. This hurtful humor is not something we want to encourage or allow in our homes. We want to protect against that because demeaning types of humor damage others. Instead, we want to encourage healthy humor in our homes and in our families.

Each family has a unique culture, and humor is one of the ways that sets each family apart. What is funny to your family members? Some families enjoy puns and plays on words. Others might find physical comedy hilarious. Whatever your unique type of humor, celebrate it and make time and space for it.

Like playfulness, humor is a great way to bond as a family. One of our favorite pastimes is to remember funny times. Reminiscing and laughing together helps to strengthen relationships. When we laugh together, we are finding humor in the same things, which boosts our feelings of connectedness.[6] And relationships are the foundation on which healthy families grow.

Humor also helps break tension in a home. Family life can be stressful and hard. We can go through seasons that are painful. Humor is one way to keep joy in our homes despite hard times.

Those same friends that I walked through foster care with have had a season of extreme difficulty. During months-long stays in pediatric intensive care with her baby boy, my friend Cayela still found humor in her day. She had been staying at the hospital for a few weeks at that point, while her husband was at home with their five other children. One day, their oldest daughter was helping to pack some changes of clothes to send to the hospital for her mom. Not really paying attention to what she was grabbing, she packed a T-shirt that read, "Trust me, I'm a doctor." (She is not a doctor, though her husband is.) When Cayela unpacked the bag at the hospital, she couldn't help but laugh at the absurdity of wearing that shirt while surrounded by a team of medical professionals. She was thankful for the expertise of those doctors treating her son. But during that scary season of watching her baby fight for his life, she was still able to laugh. God's gift of humor helped her to find something to laugh about during her family's season of hardship.

Our families face hard things. Our children will face hard things. And humor is one of the ways God enables us to cope with hardship— we don't deny what is hard. Like Cayela, we acknowledge it and grieve as needed, but we can still find the funny.

What keeps us from finding the funny?

We tend to take life too seriously. I know I do. When I am particularly stressed and under a deadline my sense of humor fizzles quickly. I get so caught up in all the things I "must get done" that I lose perspective. I easily forget that it is God's strength alone that enables me to do all those things. Tackling my to-do list in my own strength is a surefire way to get overwhelmed and lose the ability to laugh. I lose sight of the blessing of my family when I focus on the drudgery of the day-to-day. When we don't have a cheerful attitude, it becomes difficult for humor to flourish.

Sometimes it's not that we don't want to find humor, it's just that we forget. We can get so distracted, moving from one thing to another, that we forget to take the time to enjoy the journey. We will always have plenty of things to occupy our family's time, but we can decide to find the fun along the way.

How do we encourage humor in our homes?

Much like playfulness, every family's sense of humor is unique. What makes your family break out into laughter? Is your family "punny" like mine—always finding some way to weave a pun into a story? Maybe your family enjoys watching comedies and then sprinkling those movie quotes into conversations to spark laughter. Maybe you have a practical jokester in the family, like John, who is always ready to pull the next prank. Have a family discussion about humor. Explain why it's so good for everyone to laugh and then make plans for more fun. Talk about what makes your family laugh, then decide to do more of that together. This takes intention and possibly a change in attitude.

Chapter 13

Joy

My daughter gripped the handlebars with tight, shaky fingers. Determined that today would be the day she would conquer her fear, she was ready to ride her bike without training wheels. I was right there beside her, reassuring her that I would stay next to her the whole time. Quick to reinforce the fact that I believed in her, I reminded her that she had practiced and was ready to do this. She took a breath. And then as if to put it off longer, took another breath, readjusting her grip. She looked back at me as I held on to the back of the bike seat and grinned. She decided she was ready. Kicking up onto the pedals, she took off.

My grip on the bike seat was firm and secure. Jogging to keep up with her eager pedaling, I reminded her between breaths she could do it. Then, I told her it was time for me to let go. And I did. I kept running alongside her, and she kept pedaling, beaming with pride. That is, until she stopped pedaling and gravity took over. The bike leaned and so did she. I grabbed hold of her as she fell, and the bike crashed into the grass.

Disappointment and frustration spread across her face. "That's okay," I said. "Let's do it again."

And so, we began again. Firm grip on the handlebars, deep breaths, encouraging smiles, and promises that I would be right there. This pattern repeated over and over. The sun was beginning to set. My legs and lungs reminded me that I was out of shape. Maybe we should call it a night. "Are you ready to stop for the day?" I asked, hopeful. "One more try, Mom," she pleaded. I wanted to get started on dinner. John was going to be home soon, and the house needed to be picked up. I'm pushing forty and this was exhausting. But in the moment, I chose to take the time to let her keep practicing.

Again, we did the same routine, but this time when I let go, she smiled and it clicked. She finally got the feel for the balance of riding her bike. Eventually, I stopped jogging next to her. I rushed into the house calling the siblings outside. They had been out front at the beginning of this adventure but had slowly trickled inside, bored, ready to do something else. But when I ran in with the news that their sister had gotten the hang of it, that she was riding her bike by herself, they came running to cheer her on. We were all so excited!

I took a video to share the moment with the grandparents. I knew they would all want to celebrate with us on this big occasion. It was worth celebrating. She had learned to ride her bike, and she'd experienced the joy of learning something new!

WHAT IS JOY?

This is the joy of learning something new. Armstrong defines joy as a feeling deep inside when a new connection is made, a new insight obtained, or a new skill mastered.[1] I like to think of his definition of joy like the aha moment when things click, and we find satisfaction or pride in gaining this new understanding or achievement. We were created by God to experience this joy each time we learn something new and significant to us. Of course, we are created for another deeper, lasting joy, but for now let's think about the learning kind of joy.

Have you taught a child a new skill? Whether it is learning to read, memorizing multiplication tables, or tying their shoes, you've probably witnessed the moment when it suddenly clicks, and they understand. It may seem like a switch was flipped, and a light bulb came on. The reality, however, is much more complicated. God created the masterpiece of our brains to rely on millions of synapses and neurons firing. The way our brain stores, sorts, and retrieves information is fascinating. The moment our children finally "get it," their brains are flooded with all sorts of feel-good chemicals, and they experience joy.

Cognitive psychologists study this phenomenon, which they call insight,[2] the understanding that occurs when new connections are made. Through neuroimaging, neuroscientists can see areas of the brain light up as those aha moments happen in real time. And I love how science reflects what God created with intention and good purpose!

When we experience those moments of understanding, we experience a boost in our mood. God created humanity with this built-in reward system for learning! As our children explore the world around them, get creative in solving problems, and begin to understand a situation or problem in a new way, they experience good feelings that reinforce those behaviors. This encourages them to continue to learn and grow even more.

We can enhance that joy by celebrating their accomplishments, adding even more positive feelings to the learning experience. The same way we celebrated my daughter learning to ride her bike, we can get excited for our children as they experience these aha moments. My daughter experienced joy over learning something new because of that built-in reward system God created, and her joy was amplified by our family's excitement. Because of this experience, she is even more willing to try other new, challenging, or scary things. The eagerness to continue to learn more and experience that joy once again is built right into us by our loving Creator!

Even when they are "done" with school, we want our children to continue to experience this joy throughout their lives. We must cultivate this joy as much as we can, even when it is not convenient, so that they will be lifelong lovers of learning.

What prevents children from experiencing and maintaining joy?

As with all the other qualities, we cannot encourage what we do not model. If our children do not see joy in us, a love of learning and excitement when we learn something new, they will be less likely to seek this out for this themselves.

Another way we may unintentionally discourage this joy is by not joining with them in their excitement. If they share something they learned and we don't take the time to listen and show genuine interest, then they will most likely not want to share other exciting things with us in the future. They may internalize the message that the things they get excited about and the little things that bring them joy may not be worth getting excited about in the first place.

Life is busy, and we can forget to take the time to slow down and pay attention to the things that bring our children joy. I know I am guilty of half-listening as my son tells me about some new skill he has mastered in a video game. It is not always convenient to stop, make eye contact, and smile as he shares what new thing he has learned. But if we do not prioritize these interactions, we will inadvertently extinguish the flame of joy in our children.

Another potential joy extinguisher is making learning a chore or a checklist. I don't know about you, but whenever I've had to read something that has been assigned by a certain due date, it sucks the joy right out of reading. And I am a self-proclaimed book nerd! I love to read. But when it becomes a chore instead of a choice, reading loses its spark for me. I know that is true for our children too.

I'm not advocating that schoolwork or assignments should never be a responsibility our children must complete. We want our children to become hard workers who finish tasks with diligence, even tasks they do not want to do. But I do believe that if we want to encourage joy, then we should not make learning only about school assignments. Learning should be for the enjoyment of it. Again, if the goal is to encourage lifelong learning, our focus should be on all the little ways we can learn each day. God provides ample opportunities!

How do we encourage joy?

Give children plenty of opportunities to experience joy in their own ways. Point out occasions for them to use their creativity and innovation to solve problems, then watch them experience the mood boosting benefits of the aha moments! As we do this, the reward system hardwired in all of us will reinforce these great patterns. Pay attention to what interests your children and allow them to explore those interests. Celebrate alongside them as they find joy in learning, just like we all celebrated with Ella as she learned to ride her bike. Listen attentively as they share with you what new thing they have discovered. Take the time to ask good questions. Don't forget to talk about what you're enjoying learning as well. The joy of learning is contagious!

ULTIMATE JOY

I can't write a chapter on joy and only focus on the joy of learning, because there is another joy—a deeper, longer lasting joy that we experience as Christians. This true joy begins when something clicks; when the truth of the gospel connects with our hearts and minds. When we understand the truth of who Jesus Christ really is, the Son of God who came to earth to rescue fallen and broken humanity, then we are reconciled back into relationship with our Creator God. When we understand who we really are apart from Him, stuck in our sinfulness and unable to bridge the gap between ourselves and a holy God, then we experience the true joy that comes from a relationship with God. This kind of joy is not the same as happiness or even contentment but a deep sense of peace and comfort knowing the God of the Bible has your life in His capable, loving, powerful hands, no matter what.

That is a joy that I possess, and I pray that you do too. It is the truest, purest joy that I pray my children and your children experience! All the creativity, inventiveness, wonder, imagination, wisdom, or curiosity in the world will never shape our children like a relationship with the Creator of the universe. When we allow God to take up residence in our hearts and lives, He will use it all to further His purposes for His glory, and it will be a beautiful thing!

You Can Do It!

I hope that as you have read this book you feel hopeful and encouraged! Have you seen yourself, your family, or your child in these pages? I pray that you were able to evaluate your family's priorities and together decide that you are willing to live inconveniently.

The qualities we talked about throughout this book are wonderful, life-enriching, and all intertwined and interdependent upon each other. We possess all twelve of these traits, some more than others. It is our responsibility as parents to cultivate and activate them. May you be inspired to do just that!

As you make room for wonder, don't be surprised if you discover more curiosity or creativity along the way. God created us to experience an abundant life—not a life free from difficulties, but a life filled with purpose. These qualities nourished and grown to their fullest potential will allow our children to best fulfill their unique purposes. But it will take effort, determination, and a little inconvenience.

As you prioritize relationships, good conversations, boundaries, and the overall health of your family, you will see how much space you have for even more of these qualities in your home.

I pray for you and your family as you embark on this journey of inconvenient parenting and find ways to celebrate all that God has placed in your children and in *you*. May you find wisdom and joy as you go.

Acknowledgments

This book would not exist if it were not for my friend Kathy Koch. Her introduction of Dr. Armstrong's genius qualities ultimately gave birth to this very book. Thank you, Kathy, for encouraging me to share my thoughts and experiences, for mentoring me through this book writing process, and for loving me and my family so very well.

Writing a book can be overwhelming. I am thankful my family taught me that I could accomplish whatever I put my mind to with hard work and discipline. My parents, grandparents, and my sister all believed in me and encouraged me to pursue my dreams. My parents' willingness to sacrifice so that I could pursue my dream of a college degree means more than they will ever know. I am the first in my family to go to college, and I never doubted that I could graduate because they were all cheering me on and supporting me over the years. I am who I am today because of each of their influences in my life. I will forever be grateful for the love and support of my family, the family I was born into and the family I married into—they have all cheered me on to the finish of this book.

I wish my grandparents could have seen this published book. I know they would have all been so very proud. "Mommom" would've put an ad in the local newspaper and shared copies with all the ladies of the Women's Club if she were still on this side of heaven. She loved to brag on her grandbabies. I never had to wonder if I was loved, and for that I am forever thankful.

I am blessed to be loved and supported by an amazing circle of friends. Whether it was quick prayers over the phone, help with child-care while I was under deadline, nights out to relax after a stressful day of editing, or just stopping by with coffee to chat, I am loved well by my people as I wrote this book. I am incredibly thankful for each of them (you know who you are).

I am grateful for John Hinkley, my acquisitions editor, and Amanda Cleary Eastep, my developmental editor, at Moody. They walked alongside me throughout the book writing and publishing processes. They guided this first-time author each step of the way, growing me into a better writer. I am honored to be a Moody author and to work with such a great team.

I am thankful for my personal mentor mom/counselor Linda Warne. She has been a steady voice of wisdom and truth in the midst of seasons of doubt and struggles. Whenever I questioned God's calling as I wrote this book, she patiently spoke truth, always pointing me back to Jesus and reminding me what I always knew, that God will equip me for everything He calls me to. I could not have survived this crazy season without her steady voice and constant prayers.

I am thankful for Tricia Goyer who let this newbie author call her with panic-filled questions about how best to tackle getting these words on the page while also maintaining a household. Thank you, Tricia, for answering my questions and reminding me that "sometimes things have to give" while you're under deadline and that it's totally normal to want to give up sometimes. You kept cheering me on and praying me through all the edits!

And to all those who proofread, listened to me think out loud about each chapter, asked how I was doing, and were genuinely interested in the book writing process, thank you!

Thank you to Summit Ministries and Lamplighter for providing places of refuge for writing and inspiration. Your campuses were perfect (beautiful) places for this writer to focus and put words to paper.

And a special thank you to my husband, John, for pushing me to get away, booking flights, and coordinating all the things so that I could write undistracted! John believed in me when I didn't believe in myself. I would never have finished this project without his support.

John and our kids put up with piles and piles of laundry that went unwashed, a messier-than-normal house, many nights of takeout instead of home-cooked meals, and at times a stressed-out mom/wife; thank you doesn't quite seem enough. Your patience, encouragement, and understanding through this whole process means so much to me. They cheered with each milestone believing I could do it, even when I doubted myself. They came on this journey of inconvenient parenting, whether they wanted to or not; but without them, I wouldn't have any words to write. They are my inspiration, my purpose, and my highest calling. This book truly wouldn't exist without them in my life.

And finally, my Savior Jesus and His Holy Spirit who guide and equip me each and every day. Jesus and His holy Word are my ultimate source of wisdom and comfort, truth and strength for each day. Thankful is hardly enough; He deserves all the glory and honor. "Blessing and glory and wisdom and thanksgiving and honor and power and might, be to our God forever and ever. Amen" (Rev. 7:12).

Notes

INTRODUCTION

1. Thomas Armstrong, *Awakening Genius in the Classroom* (Alexandria, VA: ASCD, 1998), 8.

CHAPTER 1: WHAT IS INCONVENIENT PARENTING?

1. Elisabeth Elliot, "A Woman's Mandate," *Tabletalk*, February 1, 1996, https://www.ligonier.org/learn/articles/womans-mandate.
2. Thomas Armstrong, *Awakening Genius in the Classroom* (Alexandria, VA: ASCD, 1998), 8.

CHAPTER 2: WISDOM

1. Proverbs 3:15.
2. Charles Spurgeon, "Trust in God-True Wisdom," in *Metropolitan Tabernacle Pulpit Volume 7*, May 12, 1861, https://www.spurgeon.org/resource-library/sermons/trust-in-god-true-wisdom/#flipbook.
3. *Oxford English Dictionary*, s.v. "wisdom (*n.*)," https://www.oed.com/view/Entry/229491?rskey=MdrDPm&result=1&isAdvanced=false#eid.
4. *Merriam-Webster*, s.v. "wisdom (*n.*)," https://www.merriam-webster.com/dictionary/wisdom.

5. Dictionary.com, s.v. "wisdom (*n.*)," https://www.dictionary.com/browse/wisdom.

6. Thomas Armstrong, *Awakening Genius in the Classroom* (Alexandria, VA: ASCD, 1998), 8.

7. Jack P. Shonkoff and Deborah A. Phillips, eds., *From Neurons to Neighborhoods: The Science of Early Childhood Development* (Washington, DC: National Academy Press, 2000), https://www.ncbi.nlm.nih.gov/books/NBK225557/.

8. John Piper, "How to Get Wisdom: Become a Fool," Bethlehem College & Seminary, Minneapolis, April 20, 2018, https://www.desiringgod.org/messages/how-to-get-wisdom.

9. Kathy Koch, *8 Great Smarts: Discover and Nurture Your Child's Intelligences* (Chicago: Moody Publishers, 2016).

10. Charlotte Mason, *Home Education*, vol. 1, 5th ed. (London: Kegan, Paul, Trench & Co. Ltd., 1906), 99.

11. Kathy Koch, *Screens and Teens: Connecting with Our Kids in a Wireless World* (Chicago: Moody Publishers, 2015), 86.

CHAPTER 3: WONDER

1. Psalm 19:1.

2. Paul Piff et al., "Awe, the Small Self and Prosocial Behavior," *Journal of Personality and Social Psychology* 108, no. 6 (2015): 883–99, http://dx.doi.org/10.1037/pspi0000018.

3. Kjell Nilsson et al., eds., *Forests, Trees, and Human Health* (Dordrecht, Netherlands: Springer, 2010), https://doi.org/10.1007/978-90-481-9806-1.

4. Paul David Tripp, *Awe: Why It Matters for Everything We Think, Say, and Do* (Wheaton, IL: Crossway, 2015), 18.

5. Thomas Armstrong, *Awakening the Genius in the Classroom* (Alexandria, VA: ASCD, 1998), 8.

6. Judith Graham, "Bulletin #4356, Children and Brain Development: What We Know About How Children Learn," University of Maine, 2011, https://extension.umaine.edu/publications/4356e/.

7. Kathy Koch, *Screens and Teens: Connecting with Our Kids in a Wireless World* (Chicago: Moody Publishers, 2015), 203.

8. Lisa Kennedy, "Spielberg in the Twilight Zone," *Wired Magazine*, June 1, 2002, https://www.wired.com/2002/06/spielberg.

9. Psalm 46:10, "Be still, and know that I am God" (ESV).

10. Luke 4:42; Matthew 8:1; Matthew 14:23.

11. Johns Hopkins All Children's Hospital, "Is Your Child Too Busy?," KidsHealth, https://www.hopkinsallchildrens.org/Patients-Families/Health-Library/HealthDocNew/Is-Your-Child-Too-Busy.

12. Matthew 14:23.

13. Matthew 8:24.

14. John 11:54.

15. Charlotte Mason, *The Original Homeschooling Series by Charlotte Mason* (Radford: Wilder Publications, 2008), 24.

CHAPTER 4: VITALITY

1. Thomas Armstrong, *Awakening the Genius in the Classroom* (Alexandria, VA: ASCD Publications, 1998), 10.

2. *Merriam-Webster*, s.v. "vitality (*n.*)," https://www.merriam-webster.com/dictionary/vitality.

3. Philippians 4:8.

4. Kathy Koch, personal communication, lecture notes.

5. Julie Bogart, *The Brave Learner* (New York: TarcherParigee, 2019), 39.

CHAPTER 5: SENSITIVITY

1. Thomas Armstrong, *Awakening the Genius in the Classroom* (Alexandria, VA: ASCD Publications, 1998), 11.

2. 1 John 3:16; Philippians 2:8.
3. Kathy Koch, *Start with the Heart: How to Motivate Your Kids to Be Compassionate, Responsible, and Brave (Even When You're Not Around)* (Chicago: Moody Publishers, 2019), 15.
4. Lysa TerKeurst, *Unglued: Making Wise Choices in the Midst of Raw Emotions* (Grand Rapids, MI: Zondervan, 2012).
5. Jeremiah 17:9.

CHAPTER 6: FLEXIBILITY

1. Thomas Armstrong, *Awakening the Genius in the Classroom* (Alexandria, VA: ASCD Publications, 1998), 12.
2. Carol Dwek, *Mindset: The Psychology of Success* (New York: Random House, 2006).
3. Jeni L. Burnette et al., "Growth Mindsets and Psychological Distress: A Meta-Analysis," *Clinical Psychology Review* 77 (2020): https://doi.org/10.1016/j.cpr.2020.101816.
4. Kathleen Finn et al., "Effect of Increased Inpatient Attending Physician Supervision on Medical Errors, Patient Safety, and Resident Education: A Randomized Clinical Trial," *JAMA Intern Medicine* 178, no. 7 (2018): 952–59, https://doi.org/10.1001/jamainternmed.2018.1244.
5. Garrath Cook, "The Power of Flexible Thinking," Scientific American, March 21, 2018, https://www.scientificamerican.com/article/the-power-of-flexible-thinking.
6. Laura Burke et al., "Association Between Teaching Status and Mortality in US Hospitals," *JAMA* 317, no. 20 (2017): 2105–13, https://doi.org/10.1001/jama.2017.5702.
7. Ashley Bear and David Skorton, "The World Needs Students with Interdisciplinary Education," Issues in Science and Technology XXXV, no. 2 (Winter 2019): https://issues.org/the-world-needs-students-with-interdisciplinary-education/.

8. Kathy Koch, *8 Great Smarts: Discover and Nurture Your Child's Intelligences* (Chicago: Moody Publishers, 2016).

CHAPTER 7: CURIOSITY

1. Michael Chouinard, "Children's Questions: A Mechanism for Cognitive Development," *Monographs of the Society for Research in Child Development* 72, no. 1 (March 2007): 1–112, https://doi.org/10.1111/j.1540-5834.2007.00412.x.

2. Gregg Behr and Ryan Rydzweski, *When You Wonder, You're Learning: Mister Rogers' Enduring Lessons for Raising Creative, Curious, Caring Kids* (New York: Hachette Books, 2021), 23.

3. Ibid., 411–12.

4. Kathy Koch, *Screens and Teens: Connecting with Our Kids in a Wireless World* (Chicago: Moody Publishers, 2015), 12.

5. Bryan Stevenson, *Just Mercy* (New York: Penguin Random House, 2015).

6. Dorothy Bishop et al., "Neuroscience: Implications for Education and Lifelong Learning," *Integrating Science and Practice* 3, no. 1 (May 2013).

7. World Economic Forum report, "The Future of Jobs: Employment, Skills and Workforce Strategy for the Fourth Industrial Revolution," January 2016, www3.weforum.org/docs/WEF_Future_of_Jobs.pdf.

CHAPTER 8: CREATIVITY

1. Barbara Kerr, "Creativity," *Encyclopedia Britannica*, https://www.britannica.com/topic/creativity.

2. Thomas Armstrong, *Awakening Genius in the Classroom* (Alexandria, VA: ASCD Publishers, 1998), 6.

3. Cher-Yi Tan et al., "Being Creative Makes You Happier: The Positive Effect of Creativity on Subjective Well-Being," *International Journal of Environmental Research and Public Health* 18, no. 14 (July 2021): 7244, https://doi.org/10.3390%2Fijerph18147244.

4. Michael Boyles, "The Importance of Creativity in Business," Harvard Business School Online, January 25, 2022, https://online.hbs.edu/blog/post/importance-of-creativity-in-business.

5. George Land and Beth Jarman, *Breakpoint and Beyond* (New York: HarperCollins, 1993), 153.

CHAPTER 9: IMAGINATION

1. David Elkind, "The Power of Play: Learning What Comes Naturally," *American Journal of Play* 1, no. 1 (Summer 2008): http://files.eric.ed.gov/fulltext/EJ1069007.pdf.

2. Thomas Armstrong, *Awakening the Genius Qualities* (Alexandria, VA: ASCD, 1998), 5.

3. Andrea R. English, "John Dewey and the Role of the Teacher in a Globalized World: Imagination, Empathy, and 'Third Voice,'" *Educational Philosophy and Theory* 48, no. 10 (August 2016): 1046–64, https://doi.org/10.1080/00131857.2016.1202806.

4. Lucky Love, "What Life Means to Einstein," *Saturday Evening Post*, October 26, 1929, 117.

5. Albert Einstein and Leopold Infield, *The Evolution of Physics* (London: Scientific Book Club, 1921), 95.

6. Thomas Armstrong, *If Einstein Ran the Schools: Revitalizing US Education* (Santa Barbara, CA: Praeger, 2019), 12.

7. Amy Pachai et al., "The Mind That Wanders: Challenges and Potential Benefits of Mind Wandering in Education," *Scholarship of Teaching and Learning in Psychology* 2, no. 2 (2016): 134–46, https://psycnet.apa.org/doi/10.1037/stl0000060.

8. Erzsebet Gulyas et al., "Visual Imagery Vividness Declines Across the Lifespan," *Cortex* 154 (September 2022): 365–74, https://doi.org/10.1016/j.cortex.2022.06.011.

9. Armstrong, *If Einstein Ran the Schools*, 13.

CHAPTER 10: INVENTIVENESS

1. *Merriam-Webster*, s.v. "invention (*n.*)," https://www.merriam-webster
.com/dictionary/invention.
2. Kathy Koch, "Resiliency #5: Struggles Increase Optimism," *Celebrate Kids*
podcast, episode 123, https://celebratekids.com/resources/podcasts/.
3. Kathy Koch, *Resilient Kids: Raising Them to Embrace Life with Confidence*
(Chicago: Moody Publishers, 2022), 68.

CHAPTER 11: PLAYFULNESS

1. Thomas Armstrong, *Awakening Genius in the Classroom* (Alexandria,
VA: ASCD, 1998), 4.
2. Doris Bergen, "Play as the Learning Medium for Future Scientists,
Mathematicians, and Engineers," *American Journal of Play* 1, no. 4
(Spring 2008): 413–28, http://files.eric.ed.gov/fulltext/EJ1069001.pdf.
3. Thomas Armstrong, *If Einstein Ran the Schools* (Santa Barbara, CA:
Praeger, 2019), 42.
4. Michael Yogman et al., "The Power of Play: A Pediatric Role in Enhancing
Development in Young Children," *American Academy of Pediatrics* 142,
no. 3 (September 2018): https://doi.org/10.1542/peds.2018-2058.
5. Cale D. Magnuson and Lynn A. Barnett, "The Playful Advantage: How
Playfulness Enhances Coping with Stress," *Leisure Sciences: An Interdisciplinary Journal* 35, no. 2 (2013): 129–44, https://doi.org/10.1080/01
490400.2013.761905.
6. Proverbs 17:22.
7. Rebekah H. Bitsko et al., "Mental Health Surveillance Among Children—United States, 2013–2019," *Morbidity and Mortality Weekly
Report* 71, no. 2 (February 2022): 1–42, https://www.cdc.gov/mmwr/
volumes/71/su/su7102a1.htm?s_cid=su7102a1_w.
8. Proverbs 31:25.

CHAPTER 12: HUMOR

1. Mark Twain, "What Paul Bourget Thinks of Us," *The North American Review* 160, no. 458 (January 1895): 61, https://ia801905.us.archive.org/4/items/jstor-25103456/25103456.pdf.

2. Brandon M. Savage et al., "Humor, Laughter, Learning, and Health! A Brief Review," *Advances in Physiological Education* 41, no. 4 (September 2017): 341–47, https://doi.org/10.1152/advan.00030.2017.

3. Dexter Louie et al., "The Laughter Prescription," *American Journal of Lifestyle Medicine* 10, no. 4 (July–August 2016): https://www.ncbi.nlm.nih.gov/pmc/articles/PMC6125057/.

4. Proverbs 17:22.

5. J. W. Newstrom, "Making Work Fun: An Important Role for Managers," *SAM Advanced Management Journal* 67, no. 1 (2002): 4.

6. Laura E. Kurts and Sara B. Algoe, "When Sharing a Laugh Means Sharing More: Testing the Role of Shared Laughter on Short-Term Interpersonal Consequences," *Journal of Nonverbal Behavior* 41 (2017): 45–65, https://link.springer.com/article/10.1007/s10919-016-0245-9.

CHAPTER 13: JOY

1. Thomas Armstrong, *Awakening Genius in the Classroom* (Alexandria, VA: ASCD Publishers, 1998), 14.

2. Nessa Bryce, "The Aha! Moment," Scientific American, January 1, 2015, https://www.scientificamerican.com/article/the-aha-moment/.

By Dr. Kathy Koch

978-0-8024-1961-3 | 978-0-8024-1359-8 | 978-0-8024-2909-4

also available as eBooks and audiobooks

978-0-8024-1152-5 | 978-0-8024-1269-0 | 978-0-8024-1885-2

also available as eBooks

MOODY
Publishers®

From the Word to Life®

Love your kids for who they are.

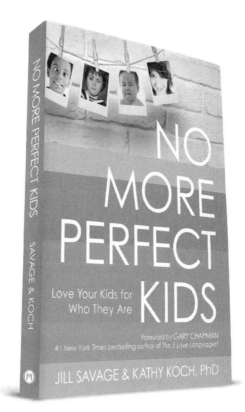

No More Perfect Kids guides you in truly appreciating your kids. It will teach you how to study and become an expert on your children, because you cannot fully embrace them until you truly know them. You'll be inspired to apply the practical, realistic, and relevant ideas and tactics to your parenting.

978-0-8024-1152-5   I   also available as an eBook

As Your Children Grow, Will Their Faith Grow Too?

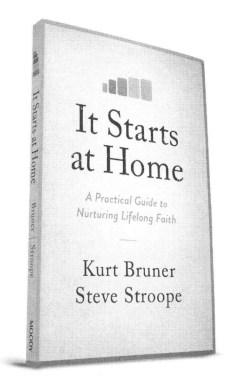

Strengthening family and home life is the best way to encourage your children to maintain a lifelong faith. *It Starts at Home* upholds marriage and family as the proving ground for lasting success. Don't let your child's faith fade to memory—learn how you can create a home that will prepare them for lifelong faith.

978-0-8024-1958-3   I   also available as an eBook and audiobook

Quiet the voices of "not good enough" and step courageously into guilt-free homeschooling.

Homeschool Bravely teaches you to see homeschooling as a calling, helps you overthrow the tyranny of impossible expectations, and guides you through the common bumps in the road. Reclaim your hope, renew your purpose, and transform your homeschool.

978-0-8024-1887-6 | also available as an eBook